In every age God raises up his chosen men, often few in number, to stand in the gap to defend the faith against the enemies both within and without the church. Willie Still was surely such a man for his time both in Scotland and indeed far beyond.

He was an expository preacher without peer and his messages will live on to the benefit of future generations. He will be best remembered, I believe, by the courage with which he defended truth within the church and the way in which he rallied other pastors, particularly younger men, to both preach the gospel and defend the truth against the surging tides of apostasy.

Willie Still stands in the tradition of Knox, Rutherford, Chalmers and the other greats who have been Scotland's particular gift to Christianity and to the world.

I was privileged to be among his friends, the beneficiary of his warm and loving spirit and his wise counsel. The best guideline I could give for anyone looking for sound expository preaching is – if Willie Still wrote it, you should read it.

Charles W. Colson
Chairman
Prison Fellowship Ministries

D1332880

This memorial edition of *The World of Grace* is published in gratitude for the life and ministry of a beloved pastor and friend of over 50 years by two of his fellow-labourers in the Gospel.

THE WORLD OF GRACE

WILLIAM STILL

Christian Focus

FOREWORD

These ten sermons were preached in Gilcomston South Church, Aberdeen, over the last quarter of 1969, and have proved helpful in the lives of some, notably the young.

William Still

This edition published in 1998 by
Christian Focus Publications,
Geanies House, Fearn, Ross-shire,
IV20 1TW, Great Britain.

ISBN 185792 411 8

Cover design by Donna Macleod

Contents

Introduction

The World of Grace contains the written form of a series of ten sermons which William Still preached to his congregation in Gilcomston South Church, Aberdeen, Scotland, in 1969.

As is well documented elsewhere, by that time his ministry there had already extended to a quarter of a century and had gone through several phases. Beginning with what he described as a 'fiercely evangelistic' emphasis, its burden had later focused on producing depth and quality in individual Christian character and in the life and witness of the church family. The instrument by which this would be accomplished was the comprehensive exposition of Scripture set within the context of much personal and corporate prayer.

Although Mr Still's ministerial pilgrimage would last for another quarter of a century, by 1969, when these sermons were preached, most of its central emphases were in place and several of them are evident here. These studies thus begin with teaching on the sinister activity of the powers of darkness, an ongoing concern of his pastoral preaching; they continue with an emphasis on practical Christian living as the fruit of the Christian character produced by the truth, power and grace of the gospel in a remarkable sermon entitled 'Paul Gathering Sticks'. In the later chapters, however, a new concern emerges. Here he was concerned with God's grace in the gospel (with what he liked to call 'sheer grace') and its powerful influence not merely on Christian character but on the deep-seated twists and turns, fears and angularities of human personality.

Since all evangelical preaching claims to be grace-centred, and to be concerned with the transformation of life, a word of explanation is necessary. Mr Still had come to the conclusion that the grace of God in the gospel was often compromised among evangelical Christians in various ways, theologically and personally but particularly psychologically. The character of God was consequently distorted (he was viewed as a policeman rather than a Saviour), and the personalities of Christians consequently warped rather than liberated.

There can be little doubt that Mr Still was at this time passing through a new stage in his ministry. For a variety of reasons, chiefly the combination of the in-depth pastoral counselling in which he constantly engaged and the help he felt he had received in it from one of his elders, a practising psychiatrist, he had developed a special interest in what one might call the psychological effects of sin and grace. In particular, as one of these sermons makes clear, he had become concerned about what he saw as a certain spiritual lugubriousness among some of the younger people in his congregation, which had displaced the liberty, joy and sweetness of spirit which was their inheritance in Christ.

So pointed are some of his remarks in this

connection that lovers of the Puritans and the Puritan tradition may find some of his statements here surprising and even shocking. He comments, for example, on the potentially harmful influences of reading *The Diary of David Brainerd*, often regarded as a great classic of personal consecration.

All this needs to be set within a broader context which is not evident in these pages. Mr Still highly valued the work of such great Puritans as John Owen, and was deeply devoted to the Westminster Confession. Indeed in this particular instance, Jonathan Edwards, who was responsible for seeing *The Life and Diary of David Brainerd* into print, was conscious of the deep melancholy streak in his younger friend's personality and the influence that it might have on those of a similar disposition.[1] Although he makes no reference to them, it is clear that Mr Still shared the insights of such tried spiritual counsellors as the Westminster Divine Henry Scudder and his own fellow-countryman John Colquhoun, that those inclined to melancholy should be careful to spend more time in the company of cheerful spirits than they do in the company of those who share their own disposition. That is as true in literary companions as in living companions!

In addition to this, there are statements about the law in these pages which might seem to verge on the

---

1. Edwards recognised Brainerd's 'tendency to despondency' as an 'imperfection ... though not properly ... of a moral nature'. *The Works of Jonathan Edwards*, 1834, vol. 2, p. 314.

antinomian (rejecting the place of law and the necessity of holiness). Mr Still was obviously very conscious of that ('Some people could twist this round and go out to say I had uttered the most dreadfully blasphemous and heretical words here ... but that is not true').

Here again it should be remembered that the rigorous and determined proclamation of grace has frequently faced that charge. Paul did in the first century (Rom. 3:8); the Reformers did in the sixteenth century (it was one of the most frequent criticisms of their message); so too did the Marrow Men in eighteenth century Scotland. In this respect Mr Still would probably have agreed with Martyn Lloyd-Jones:

> 'This free grace of God in salvation, is always exposed to that charge of antinomianism ... if you do not make people say things like that sometimes, if you are not misunderstood and slanderously reported from the standpoint of antinomianism, it is because you do not believe the gospel truly and you do not preach it truly.'[2]

Set within the pastoral context in which Mr Still was speaking, and balanced by some of the rigorous exhortations to Christian holiness and faithfulness which came constantly from him, these words will not be read out of their proper context. They will underline, however, that grace is perhaps the hardest

---

2. D.M. Lloyd-Jones, *Romans: The Righteousness of God*, Edinburgh, 1989, p. 187.

thing in the world for the human heart really to believe and receive.

Those who know and love John Bunyan's *Pilgrim's Progress* may be reminded here of two of its most brilliant passages. In the first, while in Interpreter's House, Christian is taught by his host that sin cannot be dealt with by naked law, but only through grace. In the second, Faithful tells him how Moses (the Law as commandment) almost beat him to death 'because of my secret inclination to Adam the First .... I cried him mercy. But he said, I know not how to show mercy.' Only the grace of the One with 'holes in his hands and in his side' can provide mercy. This was the emphasis Mr Still was desperately concerned to recapture in his teaching.

It is impossible not to be impressed with the pastoral burden, the directness and practicality of ministry which comes to expression in these pages. Having heard the original sermons during my student days I can still remember the awed hush which marked the end of the evening services over those weeks. To listen to a minister of the gospel wrestling not only with the Scriptures he was seeking to expound, but with the hearts of the young people for whom he had such a care, was to be compelled to struggle with great issues for oneself. Did we really grasp the implications of our words when we rose to sing Bernard of Clairvaux's lines:

O Jesus, full of pardoning grace
More full of grace than I of sin.

Something of that spirit still breathes through these pages. These messages continue to express their author's conviction that grace is still able to superabound where sin has abounded (Rom. 5:20). For grace is not merely a word or even a doctrine. Ultimately, in Christ, it is an entire world.

Sinclair Ferguson
Westminster Theological Seminary
Philadelphia, Pennsylvania

Grace is of the Spirit, and can only be savoured by the Spirit. It is there that the new creation, with its new life and power and love, makes itself felt. If we are touched there, all our difficulties of belief and practice will soon be over, for we will be able to discern what is essential from what is peripheral, inconvenient, inferior, and even false. It is the simplicity of mighty things which baffles us. Grace is such. It is not really a complicated concept, although it involves all the complications of theology, but is as simple as any absolute distinction. It is of one kingdom and not of another standing against it. It is of God, and not of the devil, it is of heaven and not of hell, it is of good and not of evil, it is of the Creator and not of the creature, it is sovereign and not dependent; it is, for all its subtle pervasiveness, of a clear-cut category, and within that category is as simple and uncontradictory as it is rich, full and profound, absorbing all seeming contradictions and even benefiting from the assaults of its irreconcilable opposite – the kingdom of evil. Yet it is as sweet as a sunny smile, as pure as a 'kind ... searching glance', and as true and unbitter as the happy laughter of a child. Grace is a kingdom which you have to be in to understand and enjoy, and once in, the whole world is different – because it is a different world.

1

TARES AMONG THE WHEAT – THE EVIL ONE

Reading: Matthew 13:24-30, 36-43

I want to speak on the question of Satan's attacks on young Christians. By young Christians I don't mean necessarily, young people, although most young Christians are young people. I'll tell you why I want to speak about this: last Sunday evening I took as my text the words of Jesus when He called some of His disciples, 'Follow me, and I will make you fishers of men'; but we got only as far as, 'Follow me, and I will make you....' We were speaking about following Christ, and how following Him meant that He would transform our characters and make us real men, men in the round, totally grown up. There are an awful lot of men who aren't grown up, who are only grown up in bits (their wives know that); not like Jesus, who was a full-grown Man.

We went on to say that Jesus called His twelve disciples to be with Him and then sent them out to proclaim the Gospel; but the important thing was that for three years these men were with Him, and it was in company with Him – and, of course, thereafter, by the coming of the Holy Ghost to implement all that they had learned in their heads – that they became, quite suddenly, when the Holy Spirit came, new men.

We then went on to speak about the loyalty to the person of Jesus. This *is* the Christian faith. It is not a book, although the Book is absolutely necessary. We know nothing about Christ apart from the Book; but God is not a Book, Christ is not a Book. I'm the last to minimise the importance of the Book, God knows; but if you don't get beyond the Book to the Person in the Book, you have failed to understand the essence of the Christian religion, the Christian faith. To do so calls for loyalty to the Person of Christ; and, of course, you can't be loyal to a person until you know him and know something about him, and follow him.

I said this also requires (it was required of the disciples gathered around Jesus) loyalty to the group. So we discussed being loyal to the local Christian community. In a city of this size, or larger, there are many Christian groups and you cannot be loyal to them all; so it is necessary that young Christians find out where God wants them to be. Everyone who names the name of Christ should join himself, or herself, to some group of Christians, and it is for young Christians to go round the city to see – I was going to say, where they would like to join – but, more important, to allow the Lord to guide them where they ought to be. This won't necessarily be according to their preferences, but according to what the Lord may have for them to enjoy (God is no spoil-sport) and what He intends they should do and give of service. And I said, you may remember, that to belong to a Christian group or fellowship, church if you like the word – it is so misused that sometimes we avoid it these days, to belong to a Christian group is something like belonging to a well-run Christian family home, where there is care, where there are advantages, but where there are also obligations. Thus the welfare of the Christian family is furthered by even the youngest; not the infants, but even the younger children have duties to do. At least, I take it that that obtains in a well-run Christian home; it did in mine. There were six of us, and we were all the better for the duties we had to do, and the care we had for one another.

I recalled afterwards what a number of young Christians had said to me at different times about the fact that they knew what they should be doing, where they should be, and all that; yet, for some reason which they couldn't understand, they couldn't get around to it. They found within themselves – having been, as they believed, truly converted (of course, that is still a question until they prove it, isn't it?) – they found an inexplicable inability to do so, as if they were becoming more and more, within the Christian sphere and out in the world too, like corks tossed on the surface of the sea. They had no power to get going. They had no clear sense of purpose. People spoke of how God and Christ gave them a sense of purpose and directed their lives. They had none of that; but rather a constant round of hearing good words from God's holy Book, as if from a great distance – like speech when the radio is turned down low. It all seemed so distant that it didn't seem at all relevant, as if one were half-doped and hearing only faintly. All very good, one knew; lovely words, true words, words that could revolutionise the world and, certainly, revolutionise personality – my personality; but so far away, so distant, so dim, almost inaudible, as if one were hearing the whole thing in a dream and couldn't do anything about it, nor rise up and follow. No power! No power to be or do what is outlined and commissioned and commanded in God's holy Word. This is why the number of conversions to Christ is discrepant with the number who really fight for Christ.

No power. Why? The answer is, as I think you will see from the parable chosen (although I'm going to turn it round a bit), that it is a work of Satan. You might as well not believe in a God at all, unless you believe in His enemy, because believing in a God, without believing in a devil, is not much more than half the story. It is certainly not the whole story.

So to the parable of the tares, the weeds (Matt. 13). Now this parable tells of the seeds that were sown by the enemy at night while the sower of the good seed was asleep: Satan working furtively in the dark to sow his evil seed. It appears from the parable that good seed refers to good men, believing men, or Christian men. The bad seed sown by the enemy, Satan (Judas would be an example), refers to bad men, unbelieving men, unregenerate men. And in this parable, the individual seed, each individual seed, is a man; a good man, not a perfect man, but a believing man; and a bad man, an unbelieving man.

I want you to think of the seed, the good seed of Christ, and then the evil seed of Satan (not equally, of course) sown in the human heart: I want to give some broad illustrations of this kind of thing. Take the parable of the nation of Israel, born in Egypt, or born coming out of Egypt, on the night of the Passover. Yes, they were twelve tribes; twelve tribes of one man, Abraham, and they were a great and mighty nation; but the Scriptures tell us they weren't really born a nation until they came out of Egypt that night. It was God's will to train them quite quickly in the wilderness and then take them into the land and marry them. Israel is thought of as the wife of Jehovah. She was to be married to Jehovah and He was to take her to His home, which is Canaan.

So at last they came to Mount Sinai and God appeared in terrible thunderings and lightnings and gave them the Law, the law of Moses, as it was called. And after He had given them that, and they were there a year and had erected the Tabernacle and performed the Levitical worship according to how He had given it them, He said: 'Now, up into the land.'

If you can visualise the map of Palestine, here you have the Mediterranean Sea, the Eastern Mediterranean, here you have the land of Palestine, and down from Galilee you have the River Jordan down to the Dead Sea. That is the land, right from the River Euphrates down to the Nile. It is in various strips. There is the coastal strip where the Philistines were, there is the Shephelah, the foothills, and then

19

the Judean backbone, the hills that form the backbone where Jerusalem is, right on the top, and then away down into the deep gorge and Ghor, which is the valley of Jordan and the Dead Sea.

God said to Israel when they came to Kadesh-Barnea, 'Now, right up by the front door, right up through the Negev (as we call it), through the desert of Sinai, right up into the land.' But they didn't trust Him, so they said, 'We will send spies in to see if it is all right.' As if He couldn't see from Up There that it was all right! They sent spies, twelve of them, one for each tribe. Ten came back and said, 'It's a fruitful land, milk and honey and grapes of Eshcol, but there are giants there, the sons of Anak. We can't go up.' But two of them, Joshua and Caleb, said, 'Yes, we can go up.' However, the people agreed with the majority; and, of course, the majority is often wrong; that is what is wrong with democracy. They didn't go up, and God said, 'All right, you will die in the wilderness, every man Jack of you, and you will stay there for thirty-eight years until you do!' And there were only two of that whole nation of adults who got into the land, Joshua and Caleb, the two spies who said, 'Yes, we can go up. We can take it.'

Now the point is this: Who blinded Israel, that they refused to do what God said? You say, 'It was sin.' Of course it was, but it was more than sin. See the strategy of it. Even a whole nation of sinners do not have a strategy fit to resist and thwart God like that. The only rational explanation of that resistance to God's will is that there was a strategist behind the whole thing, blinding the whole lot, except two 'chaps'. And so, in a sense, Israel was hardly born into Jehovah's world when she went astray in her early adolescence.

We could go through the history of Israel and find other examples of that. Take Israel in the land. They ultimately came into the land with Joshua and in so many years – 120, 130, 140, 160, 190 (various estimates are given of the length of the books of Joshua and Judges) – but, by the end of the book of Judges, the nation to whom God had given His wonderful law on Sinai, with Moses and Joshua as leaders, was absolutely saturated in some of the most perverse immorality you could conceive, living lives as filthy as the Canaanites amongst whom they dwelt and had failed to drive out. It is a terrible, a tremendous decline. Who did this? You say, 'Oh, they just fell away and were sinners.' Huh! Nonsense! Of course they fell away and were sinners, but who was behind it? 'An enemy has done this.'

God later sent Samuel, that mighty, giant prophet, to turn the nation round. Then He gave David and Solomon, and Israel saw its most glorious days. But after that they declined. They began to decline with David and Solomon, through adultery mostly – polygamy and then idolatry, because idolatry and adultery always go together; sometimes it is the one first, sometimes the other, but they always go together. Then we come to some of the wickedest kings – Ahab, for example; and, of course, God sent

Elijah to reverse all that, and Elisha afterwards – but that is another story.

We come now to Israel, declining and declining, until we come to the king contemporary with Isaiah, Ahaz. Ahaz was a very wicked king. Seated there in Jerusalem, do you know what he did? He went to Damascus, saw a marvellous altar there to a pagan god, and said, 'Oh, I like that one better than the one in Jerusalem. Let's have it down; let's have a replica in Jerusalem!' He pushed away the altar of Jehovah and set this horrid pagan altar from Damascus in the midst of Jerusalem; and Isaiah spoke against him in tremendous terms.

Then we have a wonderful king after that, called Hezekiah, who reversed what Ahaz did. He was one of the best of the kings of Judah. But, you may remember, Hezekiah had a boil, poor man, and was going to die; so he turned his face to the wall and said, 'Lord, add more years to my life!' And God gave him fifteen years. When he died he left a son of twelve years of age, Manasseh. Had he not asked for these extra years, Manasseh would not have been born, which would have been a jolly good thing for the whole of Judah. If I could begin to tell you (from Jeremiah) of the wickedness of that man!

When one reads the story, one would think – even a pagan *littérateur* reading it through like a novel would think, 'What is the perversity in this nation?' And the Bible, by the Holy Spirit, brings it out. Read it through, and you will say, 'What is the perversity in them that makes them constantly go astray, far worse than many pagan empires?' Of course they too ultimately declined; but the Roman empire wasn't like this; it went up and up. The Assyrian empire went up and up. So did the Babylonian, Medo-Persian, the Greek (Alexander the Great) – right to the peak. He fell, of course, and so ultimately did the Romans; but it is at the very beginning of Israel's greatness, at the time of David and Solomon, that they began to decline and slowly slide. That is the way with many Christians. They begin to slip almost at the beginning. And we say, 'What is the meaning of this?' Does human sin explain it? Not entirely. I'm convinced it doesn't.

Let's go on. Christ came and founded the Church: Pentecost came and brought into the lap of the Church, into the bosom of the Church, all the virtues that Christ had gained by His death and resurrection. So Paul went to Galatia and preached to the people there and they were converted. After they were converted and a Church founded in Galatia, Paul sent a letter; and if you look at some of the places in that letter to the Galatians you will be absolutely astonished at what happened.

In his first chapter, Paul says, 'I am astonished that you are so quickly deserting him who called you in the grace of Christ and turning to a different gospel – not that there is another gospel, but there are some who trouble you and want to pervert the gospel of Christ. But even if we, or an angel from heaven, should preach to you a gospel contrary to that which we preached to you, let him be accursed.

(Curse him!) As we have said before, so now I say again ('I repeat it,' he says, as he dictates this letter to his secretary), If any one is preaching to you a gospel contrary to that which you received, let him be accursed' (Gal. 1:6-9).

The beginning of the third chapter. He breaks out, 'O foolish Galatians! Who has bewitched you, before whose eyes Jesus Christ was publicly portrayed as crucified? Let me ask you only this: Did you receive the Spirit by works of the law, or by hearing with faith? Are you so foolish? Having begun with the Spirit, are you now ending with the flesh? Did you experience so many things in vain? – if it really is in vain. Does he who supplies the Spirit to you and works miracles among you do so by works of the law, or by hearing with faith?' (Gal. 3:1-5).

Chapter 4: 'Brethren, I beseech you, become as I am, for I also have become as you are. You did me no wrong; you know that it was because of a bodily ailment that I preached the gospel to you at the first (Paul was diverted); and though my condition was a trial to you, you did not scorn or despise me, but received me as an angel of God, as Christ Jesus. What has become of the satisfaction you felt? (Or, in other words, "What ails you now, you Galatian Christians? What in the world has come over you?") For I bear you witness that, if possible, you would have plucked out your eyes and given them to me. Have I then become your enemy by telling you the truth? (These people are trying to seduce you from the true Gospel.) They make much of you, but for no good purpose; they want to shut you out, that you may make much of them. For a good purpose it is always good to be made much of, and not only when I am present with you. My little children (he says appealingly), with whom I am again in travail until Christ be formed in you! I could wish to be present with you now and to change my tone, for I am perplexed about you' (Gal. 4:12-20).

Chapter 5, verse 1: here Paul breaks out into a great symphonic note: 'For freedom Christ has set us free.' Then he turns to the Galatians and says, 'Stand fast therefore, and do not submit again to the yoke of slavery.' Verses 7-9: 'You were running well; who hindered you from obeying the truth? This persuasion is not from him who called you. A little leaven (a little yeast) leavens the whole lump.' Then he says, 'I have confidence in the Lord that you will take no other view than mine; and he who is troubling you will bear his judgment, whoever he is' (5:10).

The other illustration of this is history. You may know that very soon after the first apostles and the first generation of Christians died, the Christian church went far astray – very far. And do you know, between then and now, there have been on the face of the earth, lightened with the light of the divine and eternal Son of God coming to earth, there have been a thousand years of darkness; the Dark Ages. Who did that?

As soon as the devil loses a customer, loses one of his own to Christ, he begins to try to ruin that person's Christian life. This should be told to people when they are converted; they should be told gently, graciously, carefully, but at once, 'Now, there's a devil.' How many have been converted for years and have scarcely known there was a devil? Apart from the perversity of our own nature within us, the old one, whatever we like to call it, there is a devil, and he will try to get us. He can't get us when Christ has taken us; we are Christ's and we belong to Him and we are new creatures, but he will try to ruin our Christian lives.

The story of Israel from birth in Egypt to the coming of the divine Messiah born in an outhouse, of a royal princess of Judah become a peasant maid in Nazareth, shows how far down Israel had gone. From her birth in Egypt to the coming of Messiah is one long sorry record of decline over and over again, and there is a strategy in it, the strategy of Satan; and we must learn to watch him. I want you to learn, every Christian, the facts about Satan, so that you may constantly discern him in your Christian life. I'm going to read something to you (we've written much about this) and I'm going to say again that I know of no writer outside the Bible who understands this as well as John Bunyan. We have to go back to him. I could name some modern books, or booklets, which you won't find even on the most evangelical bookstalls, because there are a great many people in the evangelical cause who don't like to hear about the devil. That in itself is a work of the devil, and is something that we have to fight against. We have been waging war all these years to put the devil on the evangelical map, and it is mighty hard work I can tell you. So many are against it. They don't see that it is a work of Satan to conceal the fact of his existence. And when he is forgotten, then is his time to begin to work. He does his best, or his worst work in the dark.

I'll read a largish paragraph from *Pilgrim's Progress*, which I quote in a book I have written about this (*Biblical Teaching on the Devil*), which illustrates how Satan can steal into our lives and convince us that we are being drawn away merely by our own sin, and we blame ourselves, not seeing that there is a work of Satan going on in our lives:

> 'One thing I would not let slip (says John Bunyan), I took notice that now poor Christian was so confounded, that he did not know his own voice; and thus I perceived it: just when he was come over against the mouth of the burning pit, one of the wicked ones got behind him, and stepped up softly to him, and whisperingly suggested many grievous blasphemies to him, which he verily thought had proceeded from his own mind. (He thought he was thinking them.) This put Christian more to it than anything that he met with before, even to think that he should now blaspheme him that he loved so much before: yet, if he could have helped it, he would not have done it; but he had not the discretion either to stop his ears, or to know from whence these blasphemies came.'

You see what Satan did? He came upon him, lighted upon his fallen nature and began to work on

27

it, and made the devil's voice sound like Christian's own voice so that Christian was deceived and thought that he was thinking these things and sinning these thoughts.

Now, there is more about that – John Bunyan again. Here is a very interesting passage. This is the story of Christian and Hopeful on their way from the City of Destruction to the Celestial city, and we read:

'Now ... they (Christian and Hopeful) entered into a very dark lane, where they met a man whom seven devils had bound with seven strong cords, and were carrying him back to the door that they saw in the side of the hill. Now good Christian began to tremble, and so did Hopeful, his companion; yet as the devils led away the man, Christian looked to see if he knew him, and he thought it might be one Turn-away, that dwelt in the town of Apostasy. But he did not perfectly see his face, for he did hang his head like a thief that is found; but being gone past, Hopeful looked after him, and espied on his back a paper with this inscription, "Wanton professor, and damnable apostate".

'Then said Christian to his fellow, Now I call to remembrance that which was told me of a thing that happened to a good man hereabout. The name of the man was Little-Faith, but a good man, and he dwelt in the town of Sincere. The thing was this: at the entering in at this passage, there comes down from Broad-way-gate a lane called Dead-Man's-lane, so called because of the murders that are commonly done there; and this Little-Faith, going on pilgrimage, as we do now, chanced to sit down there and sleep.

Now there happened at that time to come down the lane from Broad-way-gate, three sturdy rogues, and their names were Faint-heart, Mistrust, and Guilt (three brothers); and they, espying Little-Faith where he was, came galloping up with speed.

Now the good man was just awakened from his sleep, and was getting up to go on his journey; so they came up all to him, and with threatening language bid him stand. At this Little-Faith looked as white as a clout, and had neither power to fight nor fly. Then said Faint-heart, Deliver thy purse; but he making no haste to do it (for he was loth to lose his money), Mistrust ran up to him, and thrusting his hand into his pocket, pulled out thence a bag of silver. Then he cried out, Thieves! Thieves! With that Guilt, with a great club that was in his hand, struck Little-Faith on the head, and, with that blow, felled him flat to the ground, where he lay bleeding as one that would bleed to death. All this while the thieves stood by. But at last, they hearing that some were upon the road, and fearing lest it should be one Great-Grace that dwells in the city of Good-Confidence, they betook themselves to their heels, and left this good man to shift for himself. Now after a while Little-Faith came to himself, and getting up, made shift to scrabble on his way.'

Then Christian and Hopeful went on to discuss what had happened, and Hopeful said,

'But Christian, these three fellows, I am persuaded in my heart, are but a company of cowards; would they have run else, think you, as they did, at the noise of one that was coming on the road? Why did not Little-Faith pluck up a greater heart? He might, methinks, have stood one brush with them, and have yielded when there had been no remedy.

Christian: That they are cowards many have said, but few have found it so in the time of trial. As for a great heart, Little-Faith had none; and I perceive by thee, my brother (says Christian to Hopeful), hadst thou been the man concerned, thou art but for a brush and then to yield. And verily, since this is the height of thy stomach now they are at a distance from us, should they appear to thee as they did to him, they might put thee to second thoughts.'

Then this:

'But consider again (says Christian to Hopeful): they (these three rogues) are but journeymen thieves; they serve under the king of the Bottomless Pit, who if need be will come to their aid himself, and his voice is as the roaring of a lion. I myself have been engaged as this Little-Faith was, and I found it a terrible thing. These three villains set upon me, and I beginning like a Christian to resist, they gave but a call and in came their master: I would (as the saying is) have given my life for a penny, but that, as God would have it, I was clothed with armour of proof. Ay, and yet, though I was so harnessed, I found it hard work to quit myself like a man. No man can tell what in that combat attends us but he that hath been in the battle himself.'

And more: a scholar of an earlier day has written a footnote to this edition. Mason says:

'Who can stand in the evil day of temptation, when beset with Faint-heart, Mistrust and Guilt, backed by the power of their master, Satan? No one, unless armed with the whole armour of God; and even then, the power of such infernal foes makes it a hard fight to the Christian. But this is our glory, the Lord shall fight for us, and we shall hold our peace. We shall be silent as to ascribing any glory to ourselves, knowing our very enemies are part of ourselves, and that we are more than conquerors over all these (only) through Him who loved us.'

We come to Romans chapter 7. Paul is showing there how Satan and sin use even God's holy law to do their dirty work. (The devil takes up God's holy law to do his evil work.) In 7:5-8 Paul says, 'While we were living in the flesh, our sinful passions, aroused by the law, were at work in our members to bear fruit for death. But now we are discharged from the law, dead to that which held us captive, so that we serve not under the old written code but in the new life of the Spirit. What then shall we say? That the law is sin? By no means! Yet, if it had not been for the law, I should not have known sin. I should not have known what it is to covet if the law had not said, "You shall not covet." But sin, finding opportunity in the commandment....'

Paul is saying that sin and Satan are prepared to use God's holy law to do their dirty work. If you read the whole of chapter 7 you will see this, that as the sin of man is portrayed so vividly from verses 7 to 12, 13 to 20, right to the end of the chapter, looking at this portrayal of the sin of man, the face becomes clearer and clearer. You say, 'Oh, dear, that's my sin, that's my sin!' But, as you read down the chapter it becomes more clear, until you say, or should say, 'That's not my photo at all. It's the devil lurking behind my fallen nature, deceiving me, leading me astray and making me believe that I do it.'

Now that is summed up and crystallized in one of the most wonderful verses in the New Testament. (How many verses have I said that about in the New Testament, in the last two decades!) Listen to this: Paul says, 'For we wrestle not against flesh and blood (striving to be good as Christians), but against principalities, against powers, against the rulers of the darkness of this world, against spiritual wickedness in high (heavenly) places' (Eph. 6:12, AV). That's all speaking about the kingdom of evil and the devil in the midst of it. Even as Christians with Christ in our hearts, when we are wrestling against sin we are not merely wrestling against sin; Satan is constantly coming in, coming in amongst the folds of our fallen nature, hiding amongst the garments of the sin part of us, which garments, although we are Christians, are very voluminous: they are like a voluminous robe with many folds. Satan comes sidling in and says, 'Now I'll make him sin, and make him think it's himself, and he'll blame himself and flagellate himself, and say, "It's hopeless! I can't be good; and the more I try the worse I become"; and he'll never know that it is *me*.'

My dear friends, if this was the last time I stood in the pulpit – and it could be – and I had one thing to say to you (some of you have been precious to me for many years), this is the one word that I would leave with you. Get to know this fact and never forget it, that there is a devil, and he is constantly trying to work secretly in your life. And when you are absolutely perplexed and utterly puzzled about why you have no power – (you go through a lazy spell, a restless spell, a discontented spell, a spell of girning when everybody and everything is wrong, even the Lord, almost! You criticise, and you try to deal with it, and you pray, and you pray, and you struggle, and you share it with others, and you are in an awful state about it) – see that it is the devil!

Why in the world is it that the very last one we attribute all those things to is the devil? But it is! So the whole of our Christian life is a matter of detecting the Evil One, exposing him and driving him out – or, letting Christ drive him out, which is perhaps the better language. Can we do that? Well, we can do nothing about our sin and we can do nothing about Satan, but Christ has done it all; that is the Gospel. And exactly as Mason says ... I like these words: listen while I read them again:

> 'Who can stand in the evil day...? No one, unless armed with the whole armour of God; and even then, the power of such infernal foes makes it a hard fight to the Christian. But this is our glory, the Lord shall fight for us.'

The Lord has fought for us. He has gained the victory over Satan on the cross, which is the meaning of this symbol of the Christian faith, that Christ gained a victory over all the powers of evil in that cross and rose again from the dead. That is the heart of the Gospel. If you want to know the essence of the Gospel, that is it. He gained the victory over sin and the devil on the cross and rose from the dead a Victor over Satan. 'This is our glory, the Lord shall fight for us, and we shall hold our peace.'

You don't wrestle and struggle. You say, 'Lord, look at him. Clear him out!' And He will. I believe that you believe that He will. But the trouble is, we don't detect the devil. It never occurs to us that it is him. I'm constantly saying to Christians in some trouble or other, 'Have you forgotten the enemy?' 'Oh, yes,' they say, 'I forgot.' That is the work of Satan. He wants us to forget and he comes sidling in on the quiet. He must never be allowed to do that. We must detect him; that is what 'Watch and pray' means. We must detect him all the time. 'Oh, it's you, you brute. It's you!' Here, there and everywhere!

That, I take it, is what Paul means in the great armour passage I quoted from Ephesians 6, about quenching all the fire-tipped darts of the enemy with the movable shield, the shield of faith, because the fire-tipped darts come from every direction. Here's one here! Here's one there – and there – and there! That's it: Faith. But, of course, you won't be inclined to lift the shield of faith if you don't think there's any devil at all, and his fiery darts will find their mark in you and you'll not know whence they came. He is a silent worker and we must expose him.

God help us to do so, and if any one outside the Bible can help us do it, it is one man who believed in the devil more than most Christians – old, rugged, Martin Luther. Come, let's sing Martin Luther – none the worse, I suppose, because translated by Thomas Carlyle!

> A safe stronghold our God is still,
>   A trusty shield and weapon;
> He'll help us clear from all the ill
>   That hath us now o'ertaken.

2

FEAR – OR, TWO FEARS AND THE DIFFERENCE BETWEEN THEM
Reading: Proverbs 9; 1 John 4; Hebrews 4

Here is the subject: Fear – or, Two fears and the difference between them. I give you two texts. The first you know, whether you know where to find it or not. It is of particular interest to us in Aberdeen, for it is the words of our University motto. 'The fear of the LORD is the beginning of wisdom' (Prov. 9:10). You get the same word in several places in Proverbs, but here it is stated most clearly and is where the University motto is taken from.

The other text is 1 John 4:18. 'There is no fear in love, but perfect love casts out fear. For fear (the RSV translates) has to do with punishment.' In the AV, if you look at that, it says, 'Fear hath torment.' Torment – I like that. I like something that is as intense as that. 'And he who fears is not perfected (built up and completed as to his human personality) in love.'

From these texts I want to set over against, 'The fear of the LORD is the beginning of wisdom,' these words, 'Fear hath torment.' I am more than ever convinced that a great deal of the wickedness – (and I think that some might class me with some of the psychologists and psychiatrists who try to whittle away the truth of God – although they don't all do that – but I might be classed with those who seek to excuse human nature a lot of its wickedness) – I'm convinced that a great deal of violence, cruelty and wickedness are the product of fear.

But first I should have said that a fortnight ago I spoke pretty plainly about a certain subject, and last week I thought I should go behind it and show how Satan lies behind a great deal of our failures to be what we ought to be. It is the power of Satan working fear in the human heart that I want to go on to speak about this evening; because, of course, many of these Sunday evening words come from the reactions of people in particular need to the word of the former Sunday. Well, look at it this way: a cornered rat is frightened, that is why it springs. The same with what we call wild beasts. We say we tame them and they are not wild any more, which means that they are not frightened any more. It is as simple as that.

A great deal, then, of wickedness, cruelty, violence and the horrid things we are seeing today, are due to fear. Take Belfast; they are at it again there. I don't believe some of their fears are really justified. If they met, they would find that they liked one another – if they forgot their false religions! For on both sides they are false when that is what it makes them do. They would learn to love one another. But, you see, they are afraid of one another. Fear leads to the most awful things. And yet, the Word of God says, 'The fear of the LORD is the beginning of wisdom.'

Now I don't want to try to be clever and set up

an Aunt Sally only to knock it down, but it is obvious that these two fears, the fear in the University motto and the fear that John speaks about, which is terror, are absolutely poles apart. I want to ask first of all, 'What is the essential difference?' I want to dig as deep as I can and get down to simple fundamentals and leave an awful lot out, but say the most important things about this.

This is what fear of God is: it is the fear of the Lord which is the beginning of wisdom. It is a godly fear and it is all intermingled wonderfully with love. It is a kind of love, because it exists with love and belongs to love. But the fear of the Lord which is the beginning of wisdom is a fear which enables us and inclines us and constrains us, because we fear Him, not because He is unpredictable, but because He is predictable and we know His principles, and if we go against them it will be ill with us, because we can trust Him to be faithful to them.

The devil is quite unpredictable: you can't trust him. But to fear God and thus to know the beginning of wisdom, is to run to Him and rest in Him and say, 'O Lord, bless me. I won't run away from You. You are a jealous God and You want me.' He is a jealous God and He wants us and is grieved when we go away. Are not any father and mother grieved when their bairns run away from them? So we run to Him and say, 'Lord, I rest in You. I hide in You. I shelter under the shadow of Your wings; because I fear You, in this sense, that if I run away from You, there is no one else to run to except the devil.'

Now any other fear than that is injurious and disastrous. Let me give you this word which Jesus said: 'So have no fear of them (who would do ill to you); for nothing is covered that will not be revealed, or hidden that will not be known. What I tell you in the dark, utter in the light; and what you hear whispered, proclaim upon the housetops.' Then note this particularly: 'Do not fear those who kill the body but cannot kill the soul (the devil and all his agents, human and demonic); rather fear him (that is, God) who can destroy both soul and body in hell' (Matt. 10:26-28).

He doesn't want to do that, but He can do it, so we run to Him because there is safety in Him. There is safety in submitting to Him. There is safety in resting in Him. There is safety in accepting Him as a fact, and accepting, with that, our creaturehood. 'Lord, You are the Creator. You made me. I didn't make You. You made me and I'm under You and You can do what You like with me. So I'll be friends with You who made me, because it will be better if I am friends with You than if I become an enemy of Yours. Would I be safer in any one else's hands? I run to You. You know what You made me for. You made me because You wanted me to be of some use to You, some pleasure to You. Will I stand over against You and argue with You and disagree with You and refuse to co-operate with You? How could it be well with me if I did?'

That is the fear of God, then, that inclines to rest in Him and trust in Him, and sit at His feet like

Mary sitting at the Master's feet. We have been singing about that:

> O that I could for ever sit
> Like Mary at the Master's feet!
> Be this my happy choice.
>
> (Charles Wesley)

The other fear is the product of rebellion. It is the product of rebellion that stands over against God. That is exactly the beginning of any rebellion amongst the creatures of God, the creatures God made. Satan was made – we are not very sure about this and yet the Word is quite plain, I think; some people would interpret it differently – Satan was made one of the brightest, if not the brightest of the angels. Even in the Old Testament he is called Lucifer, the light-bearer. He was still a creature: God made him, and He could snuff him out if He liked!

Because angels were very important beings (not as important as men, mind you, but very important), they served God in very intimate and immediate capacities and He gave them a certain amount of autonomy or authority. Apparently, He gave to Lucifer an authority over the world, the earth; but he became ambitious and aspired to God's own seat. Now see this – this is the cause of all the trouble – a creature wants to take the Creator's seat! It is mad, isn't it? But he wanted it. And we read of him in Isaiah 14:13-14: 'You said in your heart, "I will ascend to heaven; above the stars of God I will set my throne on high; I will sit on the mount of assembly in the far north (whatever that means); I will ascend above the heights of the clouds, I will make myself like the Most High." – said Satan!

Now you'll never understand this unless you keep in mind that God is the Creator, and Satan, or Lucifer, whatever you call him, is a creature, and he wants to take God's place. Mind you, if you dare, it is very thrilling to begin with; very thrilling. Satan, because in his heart he had rebelled against God, coveted His place and His authority, although God had given him perhaps greater authority than any creature He had made. These are usually the ones who are least grateful: that is what is wrong with our nation today, we've got too much and the more we get the less grateful we are. Satan wanted right up. God said, 'I've set you pretty high, Lucifer.' 'Ah,' he said, 'but there is higher still; let me go right to the top and take God's place.'

As I said, this was very thrilling, but it was a wicked thrill and he hadn't known at first (but knew later) that the thrill involved fear, a very complex kind of fear; not only fear of the unknown, but fear of guilt. He had rebelled against God in his heart. He had rebelled against the God who made him and gave him a place of honour in His angelic hierarchy. And because he rebelled against God and aspired to His seat, thrilling though it was (and wickedness is often very thrilling), yet there was fear, and it was the fear of terror, the fear of guilt which won't confess and submit, the cause of all that damaging

41

dread which spoils or mars lives. It is a fear that is injected into us by Satan.

Well, he works first in the demons. James tells us that 'the demons believe and tremble', which doesn't mean that they are converted and tremble with joy and worship. It means that they see God. Satan has told them that that is God, away up there, and he doesn't want Him to be away up there, because he wants His place. And he wants them to help him get it! 'He is our enemy,' says the devil to his demons, who are also creatures of God gone wrong. 'He is our enemy.'

So they see that this is God, and they hate Him. But because they hate Him and are rebelling against Him, they are afraid and tremble. They are set in opposition to God. Now, Satan seduces them first presumably, by saying, 'Look, this will be in your interest. It is in your interest to follow me, not Him.' You understand the way he would speak! Then, once he has them fully caught: 'Well, I don't know if it is exactly in your interest, but I hate Him. I'll never love Him and I'll never submit to Him, and you had better come and help me. Anyway, you're caught!' So they won't submit. And it is because Satan and the demons know they are wrong that they are afraid, and it is the fear of the cornered rat that makes them hit out. It was that kind of fear, injected into the hearts of Adam and Eve, which made them hide after they had sinned. Did you read of the two youngsters who hijacked a plane to Damascus? They were terribly afraid, the girl in particular. She, a lassie of twenty-one, was absolutely trembling with fright, for various reasons, doubtless, but not least because she knew that they had done something very wicked.

I wrote the other day some notes on the Acts of the Apostles, about Satan instilling and injecting his fear into people because of his rebellion against God:

'Men do not at first intend to find themselves fighting on the devil's side against God, but the devil knows what he is doing. He captures them to fight, first in their own interests, and then when he has really got them, he dares to reveal that they are fighting in his interests. He knows that they don't like it, but they have no option then, because he infects them with a spirit of huge hatred of what, he makes them believe, is opposed to their self interest – namely, God.

Now this is the devil's great lie, and men believe it, until they are finally lost and, along with the devil – and this will be the essence of hell – they all find themselves to be disastrously wrong. Yet such an implacable hatred of God do they have, that they would not change even if they had the opportunity. This is seen in the rich man's reaction to his torments in hell. He didn't want to escape, but to have his agonies relieved – where he was!

Now where these Sadducees in the Acts of the Apostles were in the process of such damnation as I'm describing, I do not know, but we can see their whole resistance to the truth as a work of Satan arising from fear and insecurity (that is the passage I want!), which is the devil's stock in trade. Even if he were willing, he has nothing else to give to people but fear and the terrible things that fear makes people do. And you can understand why, on the

43

psychological level, the results of fear on the human personality are ultimately so damaging that they cannot be undone on earth. It is then that we are firmly in the devil's grasp and are lost. How terrible!'

Satan, hating God, makes us feel that the whole world is hostile, that we live in a hostile world, where nobody cares for us. That is the biggest lie he ever told, but we believe it too often, even as Christians. We say when we are down, 'All is lost.' But it is the devil's lie. It is a damn-ed lie, because it damns souls if we listen to it; whereas the fear of the Lord makes us, as the Psalmist says in the Shepherd Psalm, to lie down in Him in green pastures and rest in Him. You are full of fears? God says, 'Rest in Me, shelter in Me, run into Me. I will hide you in My arms and keep you. Trust Me. Don't believe him: all these fears are liars. This is Satan trying to tell you what he wants to do; but, if you run into Me, into My shelter, he will never get the chance to do it.'

This is very often what happens. Satan tries to give intimations of what he wants to do. Sometimes we dread something. 'Oh, it is going to happen; it is going to happen!' If you believe it, maybe it will happen, because you are encouraging it to happen. By that malign, perverse kind of faith, if you can call it that, you are courting the devil. He wants you to believe it, to fear that it is going to happen. This foreboding says, 'Oh, it is going to happen.' Then you are playing into his hands. Run to God and say, 'No, Lord. That is from him; it is not going to happen. It is his lie.' But we are so perverse – so perverse!

Look at Hebrews 4:11: 'Let us therefore strive to enter that rest, that no one fall by the same sort of disobedience.' It is hard to call this sort of thing, disobedience. If you are in a panic and someone says, 'Trust God,' you say, 'It is easy to say that, but if you were in my situation, would you trust God?' Well, you know, not to trust God in that situation is really sin. It is disobedience. God is saying to you from His Word, if you know it, 'I am your God; even before you were converted, I am your God. I am the only God you ever had. I made you. Even if you deny I ever existed, I still made you. Trust Me. If you don't, you are sinning – sinning – sinning!'

It may not be heinous sin, but it can lead to heinous sin, because it can lead to fear which can do the most terrible things. People do the most terrible things, the most awful things, when they are afraid: we know that. Therefore, the writer to the Hebrews says, 'Let us therefore strive to enter that rest (which God is offering), that no one fall by the same sort of disobedience (as Israel)' (4:11). Then he goes on to say, 'For the Word of God is living and active.' The Word of God is saying, 'Come on – rest – rest – rest.' 'Oh, I can't, I can't, I can't!' 'Yes, you can, but you don't want to; and you don't want to because you have had a bad injection. You have had a bad injection from that horrid creature who calls himself a doctor but is a quack – the devil himself. You don't want to. You are rebellious. It is rebellion.'

We had a great example of this on Wednesday at

Bible Study: can you stand us to expand this a little bit? It will take you into the Old Testament history of the kings (Isa. 7). This is the story: it is the time of Isaiah at a stage in Israel's history when the kingdoms were divided and the southern kingdom, Judah, was departing from God more and more under wicked King Ahaz. Because of his terrible sins, God raised up two enemies against Ahaz: his 'brothers', the northern tribes of Israel with their capital at Samaria, and the rank pagan Syrians with their capital at Damascus in the far north. These two kings and their armies came. They put their heads together and said, 'Let's go and plunder Judah and take Jerusalem.' And when King Ahaz heard it, he was in complete panic.

This is the situation. Ahaz had heard that these two kings and their armies were coming from the north, one down the other side of the Jordan, past Galilee, one down this side, making for him. At this point, we read (7:3, 4), 'And the LORD said to Isaiah, "Go forth to meet Ahaz ... and say to him (Ahaz! God says to me, Isaiah the prophet, God says to me for you, 'This is a telegram from Me to you, Ahaz, in a moment of crisis.'), Take heed, be quiet, do not fear, and do not let your heart be faint because of these two smouldering stumps of firebrands, at the fierce anger of Rezin and Syria and the son of Remaliah."

'Thus says the Lord God: It shall not stand, and it shall not come to pass' (7:7). 'What they purpose, these two putting their heads together, saying, "Let's plunder Judah and take Jerusalem," it shall not succeed,' says the God in heaven who made them all.

Then look at the second half of verse 9: 'If you will not believe (that it shall not come to pass, that these two wicked peoples in the north who are frightening you will not come near you), surely you shall not be established.' That is to say, if you don't believe, you won't be calm. You won't be fortified in your own personality. 'It is all right, let them threaten, let them send their letters, let them send their envoys, let them besiege Jerusalem. I don't care. God says they're not going to come in here.'

Are you applying this to yourselves? I want you to do that: that is the whole point. Isaiah 7:10: 'Again the LORD spoke to Ahaz ...' Isaiah went to Ahaz and said, 'Come on, be quiet, don't fear one bit, nothing will happen. They will not come here.' Then God sent another message – whether it was directly to Ahaz in his own heart, or whether it was through the prophet (I expect it was through the prophet) – He said to Ahaz the king, 'Ask a sign of the LORD your God; let it be deep as Sheol or high as heaven.' 'If you can't believe, if you find it too difficult to believe, ask God for a sign that what He is saying is true. Let it be in the deepest hell, or as high as heaven, but ask for a sign from God.'

If you are in a great state and you say, 'Oh, I can't believe and I can't be calm. It is going to happen. Nothing you say can dispel it from my mind; it is going to happen'; well, ask God for a sign, a token, something you can see or hold on to. We may do that, humbly and reverently, not demanding, but asking. God himself said, 'Ask for a sign, Ahaz, ask Me for a sign. If your panic is a real panic, ask me for a sign.' It is my guess that Ahaz had another thought in mind already, and we are coming to that, but Ahaz said (Isa. 7:12), 'I will not ask.' (I think this must have been through Isaiah, because he speaks of the Lord in the third person.) Ahaz said, 'I will not ask, and I will not put the LORD to the test.' He thought he was being very religious, I'm sure, when he said that. He was too reverent and humble to ask God for a sign, but it was because he had another thought in mind. Do you know what it was? He wanted to send to the great emperor of Assyria (don't confuse Syria with Assyria), he wanted to send to him and say, 'Hey, you great lumbering brute, come and frighten these two chaps for me.'

This is what Isaiah and God feared he would do, because ultimately Assyria came and swallowed the northern kingdom, holus-bolus, in its totality. Then the great empire which followed the Assyrian came and swallowed the southern one and they went into captivity. So Ahaz is really courting disaster when he invites the king of Assyria to come and help him against these two, for God is saying, 'Don't fear. I'll keep them back. Don't ask the king of Assyria; don't ask a man to help you when I am here.' 'Do you mean to say,' says the LORD to him, 'you would turn your back on Me and ask him to help you?' Mercy on us. What have things come to!

Yet we do that all the time. We run to this one

and that one and say, 'What do you think? What do you think?' As if there wasn't a God in heaven and a God's Book on our shelves. But Ahaz wouldn't have it and so the LORD said to Isaiah, 'Dismiss Ahaz; he is out of the count. I'll tell you what to do. Put up a great placard for all the people to see as they pass along the streets, and this is what to put on it – Isaiah 8:1: (Oh, it is a great mass of Hebrew!) "Belonging to Maher-shalal-hash-baz".' Now that doesn't mean anything to you, but this is how George Adam Smith puts it: 'Speed – spoil – hurry – prey'. Speed the spoil, hurry the prey: that is to say, quickly, quickly will God deal with these enemies.

Look at verses 3- 4 of chapter 8: 'Call his name Maher-shalal-hash-baz; for before the child knows how to cry "My father" or "My mother", the wealth of Damascus and the spoil of Samaria will be carried away before the king of Assyria.' They will come and spoil them, and you have no need to fear them.

But the people wouldn't have it either, so the Lord spoke to the prophet again and he put his appeal in a very moving figure. He said, 'This people won't have My message, My promise that I'll look after the king of Samaria and the king of Damascus. However I do it, I'll look after them, so don't go to Assyria, because this people have refused the waters of Shiloah (or Siloam).' (Now the waters of Shiloah in those days were just a trickle that came down round the side of Jerusalem; lovely, clear, cool water, but a comparative trickle in the dry season.) 'Because this people have refused the waters of

Shiloah that flow gently, and melt in fear before Rezin and the son of Remaliah; therefore, behold, the LORD is bringing up against them the waters of the River (catch the figure now, the River, capital R, the River), mighty and many, the king of Assyria and all his glory; and it will rise....'

You see? The trickle of water that comes forth from the bowels of the rock around Jerusalem is a figure for God's saving and keeping grace, not very spectacular and impressive, just a little trickle of living water, running water. It doesn't look much to trust in God. You can't see Him; you can see the king of Assyria. If you have a message for him you can go and see him. You can't see God. But, says God, 'Because this people have refused the waters of Shiloah ... therefore, behold, the Lord is bringing up against them the waters of the River (I'm going to send a River that is going to sweep them away), mighty and many ... and it will rise over all its channels and go over all its banks; and it will sweep on into Judah, it will overflow and pass on, reaching even to the neck; and its outspread wings will fill the breadth of your land, O Immanuel' (Isa. 8:5-8). 'Put it like this: If you yield to the fears that are instilled in your heart by two little demons called Rezin, king of Damascus, and Pekah, son of Remaliah, king of Samaria, then these two demons will wag their fingers to the king of Assyria, the devil himself, and say, "Come on you, and help us; we'll soon have him completely demolished, absolutely demoralised. Come on, reinforcements from hell."' And God could do nothing because neither Ahaz, nor the people, would rest and trust in Him, the Waters of Shiloah.

We cannot read any more, but the LORD goes on to say to Isaiah, 'Dismiss Ahaz, dismiss the people, shut the Book. Don't tell them any more, gather your few disciples, gather your remnant of believers and tell the truth to them and make them believe that God will keep them and preserve them.' And that passage goes on right into chapter 9, which has a marvellous ending. I wish I had time to go into it all, but read for yourselves the rest of that eighth chapter and on to the ninth chapter, slowly and carefully, and you will see that it leads to the promise of Christ (Isa. 9:6). 'For to us a child is born, to us a son is given; and the government will be upon his shoulder, and his name will be called "Wonderful Counsellor, Mighty God, Everlasting Father, Prince of Peace".' And isn't that a marvellous conclusion in verse 7? 'Of the increase of his government and of peace there will be no end.'

This is the way to deal with the crippling fears that terrorise us and paralyse us: run to God and believe in the rest He promises. I want to conclude by reading a letter some one dear to me has written, and my reply to it. This person says:

'It is easy for a while to coast along and observe rather than be involved in things, because one is afraid, and to avoid reality, depending instead on one's own unreal world. This has been me all my life, but I don't think I want that to go on; the unreal world is neither healthy nor satisfying and one does have to face up to things at some point; mind reforms are no use; down to the roots. But what are the roots?'

And this person gives what she thinks is the answer:

'Selfishness, I suppose. One has – and there are two answers here – one has a sense of insecurity. I don't resist as I ought, and so become ineffective and so must, however indirectly, affect the work of God that I am called to do, and I fear that, though perhaps I fear it not enough. Is it that I am not really fully committed? Tell me. I expect a great deal of others and not enough of myself. There might not be much there anyway.'

Notice what she says: 'Selfishness – but there is a lot of insecurity.' I replied thus:

'You make several suggestions as to the root of the trouble, including selfishness and in another place, insecurity. I am pretty sure that it is the result of insecurity; it usually is, and the only cure for that is to let the real and substantial securities we have in Christ and in our loved ones and friends in Christ, come home to us and seep into the very roots of our personality.

That may seem very difficult, but it is not hard to see what in fact militates against the healing process of our rest in God and our enjoyment of Him. It is that we will not accept His estimate of us. Indeed, it may be that you do not really accept your husband's estimate of you, namely that he loves you, and that's good enough for him. That you are tempted to think yourself better than he, seems to me to be just the kind of perverse compensation you seek for really feeling less than he is.

You see, if we constantly beat our breast and see ourselves as the poor things we have been made to feel we really are, nothing sweet, or good, or kind that God says to us about ourselves, really comes home. We just don't believe Him. We tell God He is a liar. We are worse than that; we know better than He does. We won't let Him be good to us; That is the root of our trouble.'

Then I go on to say this:

'That is why thrashing, either by others, or by ourselves, is the worst thing in the world for us. I think if you could really see this, the light and truth of God's sheer grace could really penetrate and percolate into the depths of your soul, and it could help an awful lot, it would even help physically, very soon.

And that is really about all I have to say, because it is so simple, although extremely hard because of the perversity Satan has wrought within us through fear and insecurity. Now, you must let God tell you how valuable you are to Him, and how dear you are to Him, how important you are to Him. He will not blow you up. He will not flatter you. He sees your faults better than any one else, but it is the One who sees our faults the most who thinks the most of us.

Take a load of that, dear lass, and swallow it whole. The difference could be seen in days, maybe even hours, maybe even minutes!'

A man wrote in the same strain the same week and I said the same thing to him, although the words were different.

'Most of the trouble with us is insecurity and the great answer to that is that God sets an infinite value upon us and the hardest thing in the world is for us to accept, really accept God's kind, generous estimate of us. He knows our faults better than any one else, and yet He is the kindest with us, nor is His kindness false or unreal. He is really kind because He really values us and we won't believe it. We won't believe it. If we let that sink into our fibres it will deal with all our lack of confidence. It will at the same time give us a confidence which is completely humble. Think about that.'

That is the answer. All these fears, these crippling, these injurious, these hurtful fears – and you know the difference between these and the fear that rests in God – all these are from the devil and have got to be marked and indicated as such, and as such refused. His intent is to destroy us, or at least to mar us if he can't destroy us absolutely. So we must learn to rest in God.

I find it very hard to convince some people in the fellowship that they are really accepted. They'll tell you all about their past. I'm not caring about their past: I have a past: I'm not caring about that either and I'm not going to dig into that, nor into yours. It doesn't matter a rap what our past is. It doesn't matter who we are, or what we are; if God has laid His hands upon us and chosen us in Christ to be His, then we have got to learn to love one another and trust one another equally, however unequal we may be, intellectually and as far as class, education and culture are concerned. That is of no importance, absolutely of no importance; there is room for all kinds. Let's have the clever and let's have the simple, and let them join together and be brothers and help one another and drive the devil out. 'O God, help us to learn to rest in Thee.'

Now I know it is easy to say that, but we have a whole world of mechanism to deal with the devil who comes and instills these terrible fears into our hearts. Christ gained the victory over the devil on the cross and He has given this victory to us, into our hands, and says, 'Come on now, you deal with the devil when he comes to you; not directly, but deal with him on the grounds of My victory. Here is My victory. This is what I did to him. You do it. You do it to him.' But we object. We say, 'Oh, but he is so strong. He will suddenly sweep me off my feet!'

Sometimes we forget there is such a person as the devil, such a being. We must never do that. There is a devil; keep him in mind twenty-four hours a day. Do not be distracted by him, but keep him in mind; and keep him at bay. As the Psalmist indicates, God kept the wild beasts at bay from David when He set a feast for him in the midst of the wilderness. David says, 'In the midst of foes, He set a table for me, and I sat under His shadow and ate and enjoyed, and Satan's wild beasts could not touch me.'

Let's get a load of this, and swallow it, whole!

3

EVANGELISM THROUGH SERVICE –
PAUL GATHERING STICKS
Reading: Acts 27, 28

Acts 28:1-10 – the story about Malta, and in particular, verse 3: 'Paul had gathered a bundle of sticks and put them on the fire, when a viper came out because of the heat and fastened on his hand.'

The text is, 'Paul gathering sticks.' I want to speak about the approach of grace in evangelism, the approach of the grace of God to those who need the Gospel of the Lord Jesus Christ, as all men do. And if you want another text, and think that one won't quite do, there is Romans 2:4: 'The goodness of God leads to repentance.'

'Paul gathering sticks.' It doesn't say that anyone else gathered sticks; I suppose some did and some didn't. There are always those, and they are generally in the majority, who don't. Aren't there?

I think of Paul working with his hands in other places and in other circumstances, and I could give you a list of texts where we see Paul working with his hands, making his own living because he wouldn't go around preaching the Gospel and making a living off it; although he says quite specifically in several places that there is nothing wrong with that. It is perfectly honourable that the labourer should be worthy of his hire, and if a man labours in spiritual things, it is little enough that he should be attended to in material things; but he himself in certain circumstances (he didn't always do it), lest it hinder the Gospel he was preaching – people thinking he was merely professional, making money off his preaching, as people have done since and still do – he wouldn't take a penny and worked for his living with his own hands (see Acts 18:3; 1 Cor. 4:12; Eph. 4:28; 1 Thess. 4:11).

I'm thinking again of Paul, so ready to help in all circumstances. Acts 20:7-12: Paul was on his last visit to the church in Troas, and it was marvellous that so many had come to hear him. He preached long, and the place became hotter and hotter. People were sitting everywhere; some were sitting on the ledges of the windows. Eutychus was there – and it was evening. He doubtless had had a hard day's work and on account of the heat from the oil lamps, he sank down in sleep and then fell right outside and was apparently dead – according to the record, he was. Paul was first on the spot. He had been doing the preaching, he might have said, 'Somebody attend to the chap.' Not a bit of it; he went.

Something else: Paul speaks a lot about the Holy Spirit giving gifts to the Church, and the gifts are really men to do different things. God gives to the Church apostles, like Paul himself and John and so on; prophets, teachers, miracle workers, healers, administrators, speakers in tongues; and amongst all these and others, tucked in neatly in the middle – helpers. That covers a lot and speaks more of an attitude of mind than what they did. It doesn't tell us what they did. Menial jobs? I don't know; but they *helped*.

I'm amazed that so many young folk who profess the name of the Lord Jesus Christ, are prepared in Christian circles to take so much and give so little. I think some of you young people are lazy. I know of some young chaps and young girls who slave here on a Sunday from morning till night, while the rest of you are so lazy, or so taken up with boyfriends and girlfriends, or whatever it may be, that you let them do it. You should be thoroughly ashamed of yourselves. 'Paul gathering sticks!' Now, the last time I said anything like this, there was a rush to get the brush to sweep the floor after the Coffee Bar, but that lasted only a week. Perhaps there was a scramble the next week to run from it! But I didn't take the text merely to speak about that, though I wanted to speak about it quite plainly. You may not care, some of you, for what I said, but if you want to be known as a lover of the Lord Jesus Christ and His follower and soldier, be careful how you behave, because a lot of people may come to the conclusion – it doesn't matter what you say, it doesn't matter what associations you may have here, there, or elsewhere, it doesn't matter how knowledgeable you may be in the Scriptures, or how able you are to argue about them – a great many people may come to the conclusion that you aren't a Christian at all.

That is the test. If you profess, prove that you possess Christ by being like Him who wasn't averse to washing dirty feet, other people's dirty feet; and like Paul who gathered sticks and, I'm sure, did even more menial tasks than that. What I'm concerned with in this chapter and a half (Acts 27; 28:1-10) – and we crystallise it into Paul gathering sticks, for it is germane to what I want to say – is the view we have of an evangelist; and every Christian should be an evangelist, and young Christians are sometimes the best evangelists, because they are nearest the people they want to reach. If you don't do it when you are young, when in the world will you do it? Do it right away, yet learn how to do it; and that is what we are to be concerned with this evening.

We want to look at this evangelist, the apostle Paul, in a thoroughly pagan situation. He had a few Christian friends with him, but the rest were rank pagans, soldiers, sailors; whether there were passengers we don't know. Apart from telling them that God was with them – that was a witness – and saying grace before he ate some food (whatever it was, possibly wheat in some form), he didn't preach one 'preach' the whole time. There is no record that he preached one 'preach' until he reached Rome.

Acts 28:1-10: He gathered sticks and a viper fastened on his arm and they thought that he must die, because he was a bad man. But he didn't die. Then they thought he must be a god. Well, that was a change! Then there is an old sick man, the father of the man who entertained some of them. Paul went and prayed with him and healed him. Soon all the sick on the island of Malta were, apparently, brought

59

to him, and he stayed there three months. They were waiting, of course, until the winter was over before they went on to Italy. I don't think that he never preached all these three months; but it is possible he didn't. But this is the point. You want to be an evangelist? Paul lived the life! And it was that which did the trick, as it is always that which does the trick. I don't mean that people won't be converted in other ways, but when they have seen Jesus Christ in a flesh and blood man, they won't backslide; that is the difference between people who profess, then slip away and backslide and those who don't. Those who slip away and backslide are those who have got the Gospel words in their heads and can recite them; but someone who has seen Jesus Christ in the flesh is very unlikely to backslide. I could reel off scores of people who have been converted through seeing the Word made flesh in some one: they do not backslide!

Back to Acts 27: The Roman centurion, Julius, is not the first of his kind. Read all about Roman centurions in the New Testament. They were wonderful men. I'm not saying that all Roman soldiers, the common soldiers, were the same, but the centurions we read of were marvellous men. They had such grace. They understood the Roman law, which was just and fair and even kindly. (I know there was another side to it, but this is what is seen here.) Of course, God is over-ruling the whole thing. Think of the centurion of the cross, the centurion with Peter. Wonderful men! This one, Julius, treated

Paul kindly from the first. As soon as he saw Paul, he was drawn to him, apparently without any preaching on Paul's part; so when they came to the first port of call, Sidon, he said, 'Look, you go ashore.' Paul was a prisoner on his way to Caesar! 'You can go ashore and meet your Christian friends.' And he did.

There is nothing personal in the record after that until Paul, having changed ships at Myra in Lycia, Asia Minor (whether he 'changed' centurions also is not clear), reached Crete. They had a difficult voyage, reaching at last Fair Havens, on the south coast of the island; but they didn't want to stay there. Perhaps the place wasn't big enough for the soldiers and sailors to spend the winter there. So the centurion said, 'We must go on, although it is late. We'll keep close by the coast and be all right.'

Now, here's a text! Acts 27:13: 'And ... the south wind blew.' Preach on that, some time, you preachers. You might read it, 'And the devil blew!' But Paul had said, 'Don't go, there will be trouble. Stay where you are.' But, of course, they wouldn't listen to him. I suppose it was natural that the centurion, although he respected Paul (I'm assuming that he is the same one although it doesn't say so), would listen to the captain and the owner; so off they went, but soon the north-easter came down and they were likely to be blown on the Syrtis, the Gulf of Sidra by the coast of Libya. And darkness descended. (There was no difference, apparently, between night and day, or very little.) They saw neither sun nor stars, and were driven, until all hope was abandoned.

Then Paul stood forth. To preach the Gospel? No! Well, not that way. Was he vindictive? I don't think so. 'You should have listened to me,' he said, 'and should not have set sail from Crete and incurred this injury and loss. I now bid you take heart; for there will be no loss of life among you, but only of the ship. For this very night there stood by me an angel of the God to whom I belong and whom I worship, and he said, "Do not be afraid, Paul; you must stand before Caesar; and lo, God has granted you all those who sail with you"' (27:21-24). I don't know what the religious part meant to some of these chaps, but the other part meant something. So Paul said, 'Take heart men, for I have faith in God that it will be exactly as I have been told' (27:25). Paul is practically taking charge, you see.

Now, at last, they are near land, and the sailors know it. They know the signs and are going to lower the small boat and escape, leaving these poor land-lubbing soldiers, and Paul, on the ship. And Paul sees it. Did no one else see it? We don't know, but he was on the spot, and saw it. Of course, God was behind it all; nonetheless, the man is on the spot and sees what is happening. So he says, 'If they don't stay on the ship, they'll all be lost.' And they cut the ropes and lost the small boat.

Then Paul said – this is great – 'Today is the fourteenth day that you have continued in suspense and without food, having taken nothing. Therefore I urge you to take some food; it will give you strength, since not a hair is to perish from the head of any of you' (Acts 27:33, 34). Here you see the humanity of the evangelist, who has a care for men's bodies and for their welfare: like Jesus had. Remember when He raised Jairus' daughter? They were all amazed: they had been going to bewail and mourn her death and they had the wailing orchestra, the 'Group' there. Then she was raised from the dead and they were all thrilled; but Jesus, the practical Man, said, 'Give the girl something to eat.' Some of our Christianity, and our sanctification, is no earthly good. It is no heavenly good either, because it is not practical.

Paul said grace; not ostentatiously, I'm sure; nor did he gabble through, 'God bless our food and make us good, Amen, pass the salt!' What's the good of that? He said, 'Come on, come on (they were pagans, terrified, superstitious creatures) eat, eat.' They ate and were encouraged.

Acts 27:42: The soldiers planned to kill the prisoners because, of course, if they had landed without their prisoners in Rome, or anywhere else where there was Roman government, you know what would have happened to them. 'Let us kill the prisoners, lest they escape.' 'Ah, no,' said Julius, 'not him, you won't, not Paul! We won't kill the prisoners.' So they were all saved and landed on the shore.

Whose idea was it to kindle the fire? I suppose it was some of the islanders who ran to make a fire, because it was cold and the rain was coming on; and whoever gathered sticks, Paul did. Then came the healing, the healing of the sick on the island, and the islanders' gratitude (Acts 28:7-10). Later on, when they moved, when they took ship to Syracuse and to Sicily, and then to the toe of Italy, the straits of Messina, Rhegium as it is called, then to Naples, then to Rome, what respect they had for this man. In Rome itself he was given a room with a soldier to look after him, to guard him; but a place to himself and freedom to have his friends, because the Romans respected the man, they respected his character, they respected his behaviour. He was a practical man, he knew about things on land and things on sea. He was a man whom people could respect and admire, and it is only people like that that people will listen to. If you are not respected at your work, if you are a shirker, shut up about the Gospel. Don't say a word until you can do your bit. You dishonour Christ and His church.

This, I want to show you, is the evangelism of a consistent, gracious and helpful life. Some one says, 'Ah, but you can't evangelise without the Gospel.' Well, what do you think some of us have been doing all these years? It is this we have been reading and expounding, not fairy tales. 'Oh,' you say, 'but we must have the Word, we must have the Gospel.' Not first. The Word was made flesh, and Christ commanded by His presence before He commanded by His words. And the Word has still to become flesh. This is what the world is needing so badly. It is needing the Word to become flesh, Christians to live the life – not perfectly, none of us can be perfect – but Christians to live the life where they are.

Mind you, there is more to it than that. You can live the life and it can have no effect because you are not believing that it will be used. But we are not concerned with that this evening. If you believe that Christ is with you and you are not hiding Him (and sometimes we do), not veiling Him, not distorting Him by your behaviour, you say, 'Lord, let my life speak.' Then you go on to be your natural, Christian self, or your spiritual, Christian self (it should be the same thing); helpful, kind, cheerful in adversity, patient in tribulation, admitting your faults, not being high and mighty, but believing that God is using your life.

This is the reason that there are good-enough Christians here who are living the life not too badly amongst their fellows at home (although that is the hardest place), or at work, or wherever, but they are not taking the fact seriously enough. They would say, 'Yes, I'm a Christian. I have Jesus Christ in my heart.' Well, what are you expecting Him to do in your house? Nothing? At your work? Nothing? You say, 'Oh, well ...!' Oh, well, what is faith given you for, but to believe. You don't sit there and be a nice little boy, or a nice little girl, and think that will do; that is not good enough. You have got to believe that Christ is going to use your life. And if you believe that, you'll live all the better; they belong together. You have got to believe.

Oh, get that, it is very important. Believe and

then speak, and when people ask for it, wherever they ask for it, as people do when they come to church, give them the whole works, or as much as you think they can stand. What I am saying is, we need the gracious, human, natural approach. We have got to believe that the Word having been made flesh, it is flesh in us and the Spirit of God will use our lives in context, including our words. Don't think we can be true witnesses if we never speak. That is not what I am saying, although some may say it is: but it is not. I speak plenty, don't I? The gracious approach!

Now, I want to show you this in certain areas. I want first to show it to you in Paul's speeches and then I want to show it to you in Paul's letters. The speeches I want you to look at are speeches in very different contexts. We are going to look at speeches Paul made in Antioch, that is Asian Antioch, not the Syrian one; in Athens, in Jerusalem, and two in Caesarea, on the Mediterranean coast.

Paul is in Cyprus on his first missionary journey, and as far as a gracious approach is concerned – this I find intriguing – he doesn't seem to have started very well. When he got to Paphos, a Roman proconsul, named Sergius Paulus, was listening to his preaching, and a magician, Elymas, was trying to prevent the proconsul from listening to Paul, trying to turn him away from the faith. And this is what Paul said – an interesting beginning! 'But Saul, who is also called Paul, filled with the Holy Spirit, looked intently at him and said (this is his opening in Paphos!

Of course, he is dealing with a devil possessed man), "You son of the devil, you enemy of all righteousness, full of all deceit and villainy, will you not stop making crooked the straight paths of the Lord? And now, behold, the hand of the Lord is upon you, and you shall be blind and unable to see the sun for a time"' (Acts 13:9-11).

But when Paul stood to speak to the Jews in Antioch, notice how graciously, how wisely he began. He took stock of his audience. He did not say the same thing in every context, in every situation and to every sort of person. Paul stood up and said, 'Men of Israel (notice the wisdom, the prudence, the tact), Men of Israel, and you that fear God (God-fearers within the synagogue), listen. The God of this people Israel chose our fathers and made the people great during their stay in the land of Egypt, and with uplifted arm he led them out of it. And for about forty years he bore with them in the wilderness. And when he had destroyed seven nations in the land of Canaan, he gave them their land as an inheritance' (Acts 13:16-19). And all the Jews sat, saying, 'This is going to be a fine sermon; we are going to enjoy this. This is the stuff to give the Jews.'

Then later on (13:26), 'Sons of the family of Abraham, and those among you that fear God (the proselytes), to us has been sent the message of this salvation' – and so on. On he went and unfolded the truth of the Old Testament to these Jews, until he came to the Gospel. And we read that, as they went out, the people begged that these things might be told them the next Sabbath. And when the meeting of the Synagogue broke up, many Jews and devout converts to Judaism followed Paul and Barnabas and he urged them to continue in the grace of God. 'The next Sabbath almost the whole city gathered together to hear the Word of God' (13:44).

You see the wisdom, the tact of this? Now, Athens; Acts 17. Here is Paul in the University city, standing in the market place, the square, speaking to all the pagan philosophers. 'So Paul, standing in the middle of the Areopagus (Mars Hill), said: "Men of Athens, I perceive that in every way you are very religious." (No insults there, no knocking their noses out of joint as some evangelists do with their first sentences.) "For as I passed along, and observed the objects of your worship, I found also an altar with this inscription, 'To an unknown god'. What therefore you worship as unknown, this I proclaim to you." (I'm going to tell you, great philosophers of Athens, something you don't know – in Oxford!) "The God who made the world (and heaven and earth) and everything in it ... does not live in shrines made by man, nor is he served by human hands, as though he needed anything, since he himself gives to all men life and breath and everything. And he made from one every nation of men to live on all the face of the earth, having determined allotted periods and the boundaries of their habitation, that they should seek God, in the hope that they might feel after him and find him. Yet he is not far from each one of us, for 'In him we live and move and have our being'; as even some of your poets have said, 'For we are indeed his offspring.' Being then God's offspring, we ought not to think that the Deity is like gold, or silver, or stone, a representation by the art and imagination of man'" (Acts 17:22-29).

I know evangelists who, if they heard a man standing up to a pagan audience and saying that, would say, 'That is not the Gospel.' Wouldn't they? Deny it! 'That is not the Gospel.' Well, you tell the apostle Paul that, if you have the cheek.

Now turn back to Acts 14, verse 15. This is Lystra in Paul's first journey, where he healed Aeneas and they were amazed. They were going to worship Paul and Barnabas as gods because they healed the man. Listen to what Paul said: 'Men, why are you doing this? We also are men, of like nature with you, and bring you good news, that you should turn from these vain things to a living God who made the heaven and the earth and the sea and all that is in them.' The God of nature, you see, the God of Creation; that is what he is beginning with.

You say, 'That is not the Gospel.' Who says it is not the Gospel? It is all Gospel, from Genesis to Revelation. Will some people get that into their thick heads?

He goes on (14:16, 17): 'In past generations he allowed all the nations to walk in their own ways; yet he did not leave himself without witness, for he did good (this is His witness) and gave you from heaven rains and fruitful seasons, satisfying your hearts with food and gladness.' That is not the

Gospel? All right, it is what Paul said, anyway; criticise it, if you dare, but it is in God's holy Word, inspired by the Holy Spirit. Are we learning?

Acts 17:30, 31: 'The times of ignorance God overlooked, but now he commands all men everywhere to repent (that is, to change their minds), because he has fixed a day on which he will judge the world in righteousness by a man whom he has appointed, and of this he has given assurance to all men by raising him from the dead.'

Some of you will know it has been said that this in Athens was the biggest fiasco Paul ever suffered in all his ministry, and it is true that there wasn't a general turning to the Lord; whether it was to do with what he preached or not, we don't know. Some think that when he returned to Corinth and said that he determined to preach Christ and Him crucified, he was correcting what he did at Athens. Yet some were converted at Athens and that is how he presented the Gospel to the philosophers. James S. Stewart thinks he made a mistake. Well, I wouldn't like to say that the apostle Paul made a mistake. He had made mistakes, and so had Peter; some of them are recorded in the Scriptures, or hints of them; but it doesn't say so here. But we have both occasions; we have Lystra as well as Acts 17.

Acts 22. Paul is in Jerusalem, having been arrested, having been almost lynched by these murderous Jews, and rescued from them by the Roman soldiers. And the soldiers said to him, 'Who are you to create this riot in Jerusalem?' Paul replied,

'I am a Jew, from Tarsus in Cilicia, a citizen of no mean city; I beg you, let me speak to the people' (Acts 21:39). 'And when he (the tribune) had given him leave, Paul, standing on the steps, motioned with his hands to the people; and when there was a great hush, he spoke to them in the Hebrew language, saying: "Brethren and fathers, hear the defence I now make before you." And when they heard that he addressed them in the Hebrew language, they were the more quiet.' (An entirely different situation, you see; not Antioch, not Athens, but Jerusalem.) 'And he said, "I am a Jew, born at Tarsus in Cilicia, but brought up in this city (Jerusalem) at the feet of Gamaliel (the great teacher), educated according to the strict manner of the law of our fathers, being zealous for God as you all are this day. I persecuted this Way (this Christian Way) to the death, binding and delivering to prison both men and women, as the high priest and the whole council of elders bear me witness." (He is putting himself on their side. He is saying, "I was once like you, raving at the Christians. I've been in your position." You see the wisdom of that?) "From them I received letters to the brethren, and I journeyed to Damascus to take those also who were there and bring them in bonds to Jerusalem to be punished"' (Acts 21:40–22:5).

He goes on at length to preach the Gospel until he gets to the place where, having returned to Jerusalem, the Lord said to him in a trance, '"Make haste and get quickly out of Jerusalem, because they will not accept your testimony about me." And I said, "Lord, they themselves know that in every synagogue I imprisoned and beat those who believed in thee. And when the blood of Stephen thy witness was shed, I also was standing by and approving, and keeping the garments of those who killed him." And he said to me, "Depart...." ' (Acts 22:18-21).

Now the interesting thing here is that Paul declares this wonderful word to these murderous Jews in Jerusalem who are just straining to tear him limb from limb. He is standing there declaring the truth of God, the holy Gospel, and all about his conversion and, going on from there, he is about to name the most odious name to the Jews in the whole wide world; he is going to say that God is sending him to the 'Gentiles'; but he keeps that word 'Gentiles' to the very last, to try to win them. He didn't, of course; but the wisdom of it! Quoting the Lord, he says, 'Depart; for I will send you far away to the Gentiles' (22:21). Up to this word, they listened to him; then they lifted up their voices and said, 'Away with such a fellow from the earth! For he is not fit to live' (22:22). But you see the point? He kept back that odious but necessary word to the very last moment.

Chapter 24. Now we are at Caesarea, Paul's last place in the Holy Land. Tertullus, the lawyer, has been sent down from Jerusalem to speak against Paul before the Roman governor. And Tertullus is a flowery speaker, as you can see from verses 2-8. 'Since through you we enjoy much peace and since by your provision, most excellent Felix, reforms are introduced on behalf of this nation, in every way and everywhere we accept this with all gratitude.' (I wonder what he was thinking while he was saying this.) 'But, to detain you no further, I beg you in your kindness to hear us briefly (well, well!). For we have found this man a pestilent fellow, an agitator among all the Jews throughout the world, and a ringleader of the sect of the Nazarenes. He even tried to profane the temple, but we seized him. By examining him yourself you will be able to learn from him about everything of which we accuse him.' He turns from smarming Felix to reviling Paul. I don't think that would have impressed the Roman governor, do you?

'The Jews also joined in the charge, affirming that all this was so. And when the governor had motioned to him to speak, Paul replied: (No flattery!) "Realising that for many years you have been judge over this nation, I cheerfully make my defence. As you may ascertain, it is not more than twelve days since I went up to worship at Jerusalem; and they did not find me disputing with anyone or stirring up a crowd" ...' and so on, and on (Acts 24:9-21). Wisdom, balance, grace, respect. Here is a man who knows how to conduct himself in every circumstance and make the best of every opportunity.

Acts 26. Now he is speaking at Caesarea before King Agrippa and the new governor, Festus. 'Agrippa said to Paul, "You have permission to speak for yourself." Then Paul stretched out his hand and made his defence: "I think myself fortunate that it is before you, King Agrippa, I am to make my defence today against all the accusations of the Jews, because you are especially familiar with all customs and controversies of the Jews; therefore I beg you to listen to me patiently. My manner of life from my youth, spent from the beginning among my own nation and at Jerusalem, is known by all the Jews. They have known for a long time, if they are willing to testify, that according to the strictest party of our religion I have lived as a Pharisee. And now I stand here on trial for hope in the promise made by God to our fathers, to which our twelve tribes hope to attain, as they earnestly worship night and day. And for this hope I am accused by Jews, O King!"' (26:1-7).

Then he goes on, 'Why is it thought incredible by any of you that God raises the dead?' (Acts 26:8) And he proceeds with his case, graciously, convincingly, and tells again the story of his conversion as in chapter 22, until at verse 19 of chapter 26 he says: 'Wherefore, O King Agrippa (when Christ appeared to me on the Damascus road), I was not disobedient to the heavenly vision, but declared first to those at Damascus, then at Jerusalem and throughout all the country of Judea, and also to the Gentiles, that they should repent and turn to God and perform deeds worthy of their repentance. For this reason the Jews seized me in the temple and tried to kill me. To this day I have had the help that comes from God, and so I stand here testifying both to small and great, saying nothing but what the prophets and Moses said would come to pass: that the Christ must suffer, and that, by being the first to rise from the dead, he would proclaim light both to the people (the Jews) and to the Gentiles' (19-23). As he made his defence, the power of the Holy Spirit was so absolutely tremendous that Festus said, 'Paul, you are mad, your great learning is turning you mad' (29): he was cut to the heart with conviction of sin. And Agrippa said, 'In a short time you think to make me a Christian!' (28).

You see the wisdom? You say, 'I'm not an apostle Paul, I couldn't be like him.' But are you prepared to learn from him? That is the point.

I could go over many of Paul's letters – which are, of course to Christians – but the grace of his approach is evident in every one. Look at First Corinthians. Paul lashed these Corinthians as he lashed no other Christians, but see how he began to thrash and dress down and give them such a licking as they had never had in their lives. This is how he began the letter; can you credit it? Some would think he was insincere. 1 Corinthians 1:4-7: 'I give thanks to God always for you because of the grace of God which was given you in Christ Jesus, that in every way you were enriched in him with all speech and all knowledge – even as the testimony to Christ was confirmed among you – so that you are not lacking in any spiritual gift....'

Had there been time, I could have read Romans, Corinthians, Ephesians, Colossians, First and Second Thessalonians, Second Timothy, Philemon – the whole lot! Men and women, it is the love of Christ that saves; nothing else. It is the love of Christ that saves Christians, and Christians need very much to be saved, for there are many salvations. If you are saved (what you call saved), you are only begun to be saved; it is a process as well as a crisis, with a consummation. It is love alone that saves.

Now what I am concerned with is not so much that certain words should not be used in one's approach to people; it is more the attitude in which they are used. I think if the attitude were different, the words used would often be different. It is compassion that moves. It is grace, not hammerings, that melts hearts and produces sorrow and repentance.

There is a certain gracious approach to the unconverted. Turn to Jesus Himself. Jesus, far more than any evangelist, is seeking to produce conviction of sin in people He meets, and He succeeds where many don't because He begins the right way. It is the goodness of God that leads to repentance; and He is soon dealing with the Woman of Samaria's sin; He is soon dealing with Zacchaeus' sin; and dealing with the sin of the woman taken in adultery. See how gracious He is to her, His compassion. I looked at the references in the Gospels to our Lord's compassion. After He had healed the woman with the issue of blood, Jairus' daughter and the demoniac, the crowds came, and it says (Matt. 9:36), 'He had compassion on the crowds.'

He fed the five thousand because He had compassion on their bodies (Matt. 14:15-21; Mark 6:35-44). He had fed their souls and then He gave them bread for their bodies, because He had compassion on them, they had come such a long distance. He fed the four thousand (Matt. 15:32-39; Mark 8:1-10). He had compassion on the blind man at Jericho (Mark 10:46-52). It says most beautifully in the Gospel according to Mark that He loved the rich young ruler (Mark 10:21). Some Christians couldn't love a rich young ruler, they would sneer at him. The father of the prodigal, when he saw his son, had compassion on him, and ran and fell on his neck and kissed him (Luke 15:20). The Good Samaritan, when he saw the man whom the priest and the Levite had ignored, in distress and wounded and robbed, he had compassion on him (Luke 10:33).

Why, even the Old Testament is full of this. Listen to this from Exodus, the Lord speaking to Moses after the sin of the Golden Calf. 'The LORD passed before him and proclaimed, "The LORD, the LORD, a God merciful and gracious, slow to anger, and abounding in steadfast love and faithfulness, keeping steadfast love for thousands, forgiving iniquity and transgression and sin"' (Exod. 34:6, 7a).

Or, take the Lord speaking through Hosea to wayward Israel. 'How can I give you up, O Ephraim!' 'I can't have you, because you are so unclean and unholy. I can't take you to my breast, but how can I give you up!' The Lord in heaven is weeping, 'How can I hand you over, O Israel! How can I make you like Admah!' You know what Admah is? Admah is one of the other cities like Sodom and Gomorrah, 'How can I make you like Admah! How can I treat you like Zeboim! My heart recoils within me (from doing that), my compassion grows warm and tender. I will not execute my fierce anger, I will not again destroy Ephraim; for I am God and not man' (Hos. 11:8, 9).

Now we are to stop blasting sinners. That is not the way. That is not Jesus' way and it is not going to be our way.

A brother was reminding me that we once preached hell here, morning and evening, for six weeks. We know all about that, that we get a name for preaching hell and judgment, but let us do it with tears, not with hard steely voices. Unless you can weep over sinners, don't you tell them about hell and judgment. Was it Murray McCheyne who said to Andrew Bonar, when they were walking together on a Monday morning, discussing Sunday, 'I was preaching on hell, yesterday'? The other said, 'Did God give you grace to preach it tenderly?'

If He doesn't, don't let's do it at all until we can. Have you got the message? I'm tired harping on it. I don't want to say it again for a long time. I'm tired of it, but it will have to be said again unless we learn. Oh God, give us compassion for the lost, and then, I believe, many will be found.

4

CARING FOR OTHERS –
DIVES AND LAZARUS
Reading: Luke 16:19-31; Matthew 25:31-46

The poor man wasn't in heaven because he was poor, but because he had been a faithful son of Abraham; and because he had been a faithful son of Abraham, his condition in heaven is marvellously reversed from that on earth. The converse is true, as you would expect; the rich man wasn't in hell because he was rich. There are men whom God has appointed to be rich and has given power to be moneyed, in order that they might honour God and serve His cause; and they do, some of them; but it is a tremendous temptation and many fall by the wayside. Let us say in the first instance, although there is more to it than this, the rich man was in hell because he did not care for his brother Jew: whether he was a beggar or not, he was a man in need and he did not care for him. He was utterly selfish, lived absolutely for himself, and was as hard as nails, as far as the piece of quivering flesh was concerned which blemished the entrance to his (doubtless) palatial home.

Now of course, there has to be a levelling up. It would be a bad thing if there wasn't a levelling up in the world which comes after this one, for dear me, there is tremendous need for that, a place where all wrongs will be righted. Aren't you glad there is a judgment in heaven and hell? If you are not, if you are not glad about both, then there is something wrong with you as a Christian. You may think you are very compassionate and very gracious and all that, but you aren't really, you are just ignorant. You are saying, 'Let all that lot get into heaven; they will not make that much of a mess!' You don't know. You don't know that the spirit of their father, the one who has made the mess of the world, is still in them. Yes, thank God, there must be a squaring up; and what a comfort that is to all who hate the injustices and wrongs of this world.

But it seems to me that it is just a step from not caring for your brother – perhaps it is hardly a step, but something cankered and vile has begun in your heart and you have ceased to care for him – I say it is just a step, or scarcely a step from not caring to despising and ultimately wanting to destroy him as Cain sought to destroy, and indeed did destroy, mortally speaking, his brother Abel. Cain was jealous of his brother, righteous Abel, and ultimately slew him.

Look at what John says about this (1 John 3:11-18): 'For this is the message which you have heard from the beginning, that we should love one another, and not be like Cain who was of the evil one and murdered his brother. And why did he murder him? Because his own deeds were evil and his brother's righteous.' (He was jealous, the devil was jealous of God and started all that.) 'Do not wonder, brethren, that the world hates you. We know that we have passed out of death into life, because we love the brethren (that is the sign). He who does not love remains in death. Any one who hates his brother is a murderer, and you know that no murderer has eternal life abiding in him. By this we know love, that He (Jesus) laid down His life for us; and we ought to lay down our lives for the brethren.' (Are you taking that in? He laid down his life for us, and we ought to lay down our lives for the brethren.) 'But if anyone has the world's goods (that is, the rich man) and sees his brother in need (he saw him every time he went out and came into his house), yet closes his heart against him, how does God's love abide in him?' John says, 'Tell me where it is? Where is God's love in him? Let me see proof of it.' 'Little children, let us not love in word or speech but in deed and in truth.'

If we don't love our brother (whether our natural brother or our spiritual brother), how can we love the lost? How can we, as Jesus commands us in the Sermon on the Mount (Matt. 5), love our enemy? How can we, perverse, fallen creatures, how can we do these things unless the Spirit of Christ, the Spirit of love is in us?

Of course, we may say that the rich man was not converted, and I think it appears very likely that he refused the Word; certainly his brothers had, and it would be a fair assumption that he too had refused the Gospel. And in hell he asked that Lazarus be sent to warn his brothers. But Abraham said to him, 'They have Moses and the prophets.' 'Oh, no,' said the rich man, 'go and show them a sign and they will repent. If someone goes from the dead they will repent.' 'No,' said Abraham, who, of course, saw eye to eye with his Lord, 'no, they wouldn't, because if they wouldn't hear the word of Moses and the prophets, my Gospel, they wouldn't believe any sign whatever.' That is why people seek signs; they want to keep God on a string. They want Him to dance attendance on them. They say, 'No, Lord, I'm not coming in that way. I'll go this way if you please.'

The Pharisees and the Sadducees came, and to test Jesus they asked Him to show them a sign from heaven. Jesus answered them, 'When it is evening, you say, "It will be fair weather; for the sky is red." And in the morning, "It will be stormy today, for the sky is red and threatening." You know how to interpret the appearance of the sky, but you cannot interpret the signs of the times.' And then He said this: 'An evil and adulterous generation seeks for a sign, but no sign shall be given to it except the sign of Jonah' (Matt. 16:1-4). Jonah was three days in the fish, speaking parabolically of Jesus' three days in the ground. The only sign that is given will be that sign, not as a symbol, dressed up in a church, but what it is.

Jesus said in another place, 'Except ye see signs and wonders, ye will not believe' (John 4:48). And He might have added, which He does in various places by implication, that even if people claim to believe because they have seen signs, they are simply turning Christ into a kind of magician. 'Go on, Lord, perform! Dance for me and I will follow you.' The cheek of it! 'This is the way,' He says. The only way is by receiving the Gospel, the words of the good news of Jesus Christ, humbling your hearts to receive it; and no signs will do you any good.

That is why it was a concession to the weakness of the disciples that Jesus stilled the storm on Galilee. He shouldn't have had to do so. He should have been able to say to these men, 'It's all right, we are able to ride out the storm. I won't sink. I won't drown, you foolish fellows.' That is how kind He is to our weakness. Do we give Him credit for that? I wonder if we do. No signs! If you want a sign, if you are not pleased with holding on to God's holy Word, there is something wrong with you, and there is something wrong with your faith, your Christianity; and you had better see to it. Naked faith in God's pure Word mediated by His Spirit is all we ought to need. 'No,' said Abraham, 'no, no, no, we will send no-one from the dead to your five brothers, because it wouldn't make the slightest difference. They have turned their backs, as you have, on the holy Gospel, which you have known since a child, and I'm afraid they are sunk, as you are sunk.'

But, you may say, coming back to the first part of the story and to Matthew 25, many doers of good, who show a great deal of what they believe to be real compassion, are not converted. Yes, it is true, and Jesus speaks about that. George Macleod used to instance Matthew 25 as the indication that the test of Christians is not evangelical jargon and not subscribing to some evangelical creed, but doing good to one's fellows. And the test extends to heaven or hell. But George Macleod needs to be reminded of Matthew 7:21, where Jesus says these words: 'Not everyone who says to me, "Lord, Lord," shall enter the kingdom of heaven, but he who does the will of my Father who is in heaven.' 'Well,' you say, 'that is doing.' Yes, but look at this: 'On that day many will say to me, "Lord, Lord, did we not prophesy in your name, and cast out demons in your name (undoubtedly, casting out demons by demons, certainly not by the power of God), and do many mighty works in your name?"' (7:22). Many works of power ... that seemed to be good works, healing people. The devil can heal. Didn't you know that the devil can heal, to lead people astray? Didn't you know that he can heal bodies to lead people astray? Didn't you know that? It is time you did. Many works of power, dynamic works. ... And what does Jesus say about them? 'And then I will declare to them, "I never (it's emphatic – no never!) knew you; depart from me you evildoers"' (Matt. 7:22, 23).

It is the Word that saves; not the bare intellectual word, but the Word, quickened, enlivened and distilled into spiritual essence by the Spirit of God. It is the Word that saves, as it is the Word that creates true compassion. And see what it is in the Word that creates true compassion – it is gratitude to God. We care for others because of our gratitude to God for what He has done for us. That is what we say in the Lord's Prayer, asking the Lord 'to forgive, as we forgive'. Because of our gratitude to God for forgiving us, we want to forgive others. God has done it for us.

When people are hard on their fellows, as Christians sometimes are, it is because they have forgotten what sinners they were themselves. Maybe they never knew, because they hadn't the opportunity to have drawn out of them all their potential for evil; but sinners we are, I tell you. If you look into your heart, deep enough down, you will see that; so much so that when the grace of God comes to a man and seeks to forgive and says, 'Now you must forget it. Put it behind you. Hold up your head. He has forgiven you. It doesn't matter what the world says or thinks, He has forgiven it.' ... Oh, if you are involved in this, as I am, from day to day, and week to week, you will know it is one of the hardest things in the world to tell sinners that God has forgiven them when they have repented. You say, 'I can't take it in, I'm so ashamed.' Yes, yes, yes – but go on from that. There are some who profess to be Christians who have had no experience that has ever caused them to shed a tear – not one tear. Are they converted? It remains to be seen. Yes, it does. Gratitude to God for forgiveness is the thing, when we appropriate and take over, to some extent, His compassion and forgiveness, and say on His behalf, 'Oh, forget it, forget it. Come, let's be friends. Drop it! No more about it! Hold your tongue about it. I don't want to hear about it any more.' You don't do this for effect. Of course, you can, you can do it very sanctimoniously, and that is horrid, but if you do it reasonably and humbly, you will say, 'Let's talk about something nicer,' because you know what it is yourself to be forgiven. And with that, of course, comes a whole world of compassion and care.

But this matter has two sides. How are we to know that we are real Christians? There are some here who would say, 'Well, I have responded to the Gospel, I have received Jesus Christ, and I love Him in a kind of a way and I've read His Word, and I pray to Him, and I go to lots of Christian gatherings, and Bible Study and Prayer, and all that sort of thing.' Careful – careful! This is exactly what I am worried about, when I see so little care for others in people who profess all that, and are involved in all that. There are so very many of them and I begin to wonder how many have really been touched by the grace of God and how many are really indwelt by the Spirit of Christ, having been brought to the birth in God. If you say you love Jesus, how are you going to show it? Jesus says the whole Law, the whole Gospel of the Old Testament hangs on this, 'Love God and your neighbour as yourself.'

Someone wrote from more than half across the world in reply to something Dr. Geoffrey Dixon said here in the pulpit some little time ago. He was warning against self-hatred, and someone wrote and said, 'I was worried about that, because we have been very concerned here about people who are afflicted with self-love.' So I wrote back to the dear man (a missionary) and said, 'You must see this in context. Here is a man dealing with warped personalities, and there are some of those even in the church; and some of them, under the influence of the devil, have learned to hate themselves almost as far as to abandon their lives altogether.' What does Jesus say? Do the last two words of the statement mean nothing? Are we to lose respect, care, for ourselves? 'Love God and your neighbour as yourself.' That has its rightful place. Don't let's overdo it; but love God and your neighbour as yourself. That is the test that we love Jesus.

When Jesus and the disciples had the resurrection picnic (and I've been there, on the very spot), – after Peter had disgraced himself by betraying his Lord – Jesus fixed him with that kindly eye which penetrates more than eagle, fiery eyes – gentle eyes do penetrate, you know, they hold the gaze – Jesus set His gentle, kindly, all-searching eye on Peter and said, 'Peter, do you love Me most of all; more than these?' – Whether He meant the other disciples, or the fish, or whatever. Peter replied, 'Yes, Lord: I won't speak for myself, I call You to witness, You who knowest all things, to witness that I love You.' 'All right, then,' said Jesus (and this took place, as you know, three times: John 21:15-18): 'all right, my man, prove it.' 'How, Lord?' 'Care for My lambs, feed My sheep.' Or, a cup of cold water in the name of Jesus: that's it.

In a few weeks, on Christmas Sunday, I will be saying to the children when they bring in their gaily-wrapped parcels, and look pleased with themselves because the gifts are to be given to poor children:

'Do you know what you have done? You have given Jesus a birthday present. But why don't you give it to Himself?' Then I will very likely say something like this: 'There are rockets which go to the moon, but there are no rockets which go right up to Jesus on His birthday; so He sends a telephone message down to you and says, "Give your gift to the poorest child you can find in Aberdeen".'

My friends, that is the only way on earth by which we can show in action that we love Jesus Christ – by caring for others; and that is exactly what Jesus is teaching in Matthew 25:31-46.

We might have sung this hymn this evening: listen to what it says; it is by Philip Doddridge:

> Fountain of good, to own Thy love
>   Our thankful hearts incline;
> What can we render, Lord, to Thee,
>   When all the worlds are Thine?
>
> But Thou hast needy brethren here,
>   Partakers of Thy grace,
> Whose names Thou wilt Thyself confess
>   Before the Father's face.
>
> And in their accents of distress
>   Thy pleading voice is heard;
> In them Thou mayst be clothed and fed,
>   And visited and cheered.

That is just the essence of the chapters we read (Luke 16:19-31; Matthew 25:31-46). Then this: it goes further:

> Thy face, with reverence and with love,
> We in Thy poor would see;
> O may we minister to them,
> And in them, Lord, to Thee.

Jesus says to the sheep on the right hand, 'Come, O blessed of my Father ... I was hungry ... thirsty ... naked ... and you came to me.' 'Lord, when...?'

When the Spirit of Jesus Christ works within us to give us compassion for men, we may not know how religious it is because it seems so natural and human. We are far too religious, we Christians, far too religious; and you know what I mean by that. Surely you know what I mean by that? This self-consciousness!

Remember James' definition of true religion; it is not an exhaustive definition but it is a true one: 'Visiting the fatherless and the widows, and keeping oneself unspotted from the world.' Well? We are far too religious, far too self-conscious. This is why so many Christians need so many props for their faith. That is why we need so many meetings, too many meetings; meetings to bolster faith, insecure faith, faith that is not set upon Christ Himself and on the facts of the holy Gospel, faith that needs constant boosting.

When the Spirit of Jesus Christ is in your heart – and if He isn't, of course, this doesn't apply to you yet – but when the Spirit of Jesus Christ is in your heart and is operating, you don't sally out one day, saying, 'I will be religious, and I will care for some of the poor around me.' No, you go out and be natural. Dare you be natural? When you are being natural, are you being Christian? If the Spirit of Jesus Christ is in your heart, you cannot be natural without being Christian; it is natural to be Christian, if Christ is in you. I know there is a devil, but we are not talking about him now. Your life tells – if you have faith to believe that it is telling, of course, your life tells and people see it.

Jesus says to those on the left hand, the goats, 'Depart from me ... for I was hungry ... thirsty ... needing to be visited and you did not visit me.' 'Lord, where? When?' 'Because you did it not to one of the least.' I love the way Jesus speaks to extremes. There is nothing in the carnal, intellectual, philosophical sense, balanced and measured and moderate. He is an extremist. And because He believes in extremes, 'that-a-way' (motioning right) and 'that-a-way' (motioning left), He is the most balanced Man in the world. He says, 'the least'. Perhaps He means that the least were in greatest need. Paul says that, somewhere, doesn't he? We must care for the weak brothers because they need our care more than the strong brothers – if there are any strong brothers!

Here are two Bible readings in which the test of whether we are to go to heaven or hell is compassion. – Ah, but wait a moment – I'm not ignoring the second part of the story of the rich man and Lazarus, which speaks about the necessary Gospel; that is not being left out at all; but notice what I am saying now, this is extreme and astonishing. Twice in those passages I have read to you, the test between heaven and hell is compassion for men's bodies. There is nothing in either of these accounts about attending to men's souls. Now that is a queer thing, is it not? And I can hear some of you crying to one another over the top of my words, 'Don't let that man go to extremes and pervert the Gospel for you!' Of course not, but this is the way we care for souls and seek to win souls to Jesus Christ. You say, 'The worldling does that, with his housing and social benefits and service.' Of course he does, but it is different, radically, categorically, eternally different, because it is not done for Christ, it is done for self. It cannot be done for Him, if Christ is not in the heart. It cannot be done for Christ when there is no love for Christ, when there is hatred of Christ in so many social workers' hearts. It is not done for Christ, it is done for self, however hidden and subtle that may be – philanthropy, and all that kind of thing. It is as different from Christian compassion as heaven from hell, although they may look alike. They do look alike on the surface, if you have no discernment. But we ought to have discernment.

In both accounts we see compassion for people's bodies in their distress. This is the test – there are others, very important and vital tests not dealt with this evening – but I am dealing with this test, and not others. Some who profess Jesus Christ are so taken up with the evangelistic and evangelical round – aye, here as well as other places – that they have forgotten the fact that we have to show our Christian grace by caring for people in their situations, where they are.

Now everyone who professes to love Jesus Christ, I don't care how keen a Christian you are (and it is interesting that even those who have had the least educational background or advantages and who may have the least brains – or it may seem so, they don't know perhaps their potentials until they try to use them – as soon as they are converted – and this may be a sign that there is a real work of grace in their hearts – want to improve themselves and go to colleges of various kinds), but if you give all your time to the evangelical round and haven't a moment to show you care for your fellow men, the lost, by ministering in some way to their needs, what is the use of that?

Many of you young folks should find some old man or woman to visit once a week, to spend an hour or two with them. I don't care how busy you are; some of you study too long at a stretch and strain your minds. An hour of such visiting in between times would refresh you and you would go back to your studies far better able to cope. Come on now! You profess the name of Jesus Christ? Well, follow His Word. It is not my word. It is His word. Let's see some love of Jesus in love of men, both Christian brothers and those not Christian brothers, or not yet – the lost.

5

PROPITIATION
Reading: Romans 1:18; 1 John 2:2, 4:10

I told you what the text was: Romans 1:18. It leads
to many things, but we'll take the first part of the
verse only, and you will see why later on. Paul has
been saying that he is not ashamed of the Gospel: it
is the power of God to salvation, to the Jew first and
also to the Gentile (Rom. 1:16); in the Gospel, the
saving righteousness of God is revealed from faith
to faith; as it is written in Habakkuk 2:4, 'The just
shall live by faith.' Then he goes on to say, 'For the
wrath of God is revealed from heaven against all
ungodliness and unrighteousness of men.'

Some modern scholars who work on the
Scriptures, and teach others how they should read
them and what they should preach and teach about
them, are very unhappy with this word, 'wrath',
because they don't believe it applies to God at all.
They think that that word, along with the word
practically synonymous with it, 'anger', ought not
to be applied to the God of the Bible and of the
Gospel, the Father of our Lord Jesus Christ, the
God who is love. They think to speak about the
wrath or anger of God at all, suggests ideas that
rank pagans have about an angry God, with the
suggestion – it is perhaps more in their minds than in
other people's minds – that God is liable to get into a

bad temper and be capricious in His anger; vindictive indeed, arbitrary and unethical. But the Bible tells us there is such a thing as righteous wrath, righteous anger. Why shouldn't God's wrath (which Paul speaks about here and the Bible speaks about in so many places – more places than you might imagine) be righteous wrath? Surely we can assume that when the Bible says God is angry, that God is wrathful with wicked men, it doesn't mean He is in a bad temper, but that His anger and wrath are righteous. That is why in the second portion of Romans which we read, while the RSV reads the word 'expiate' in 3:25, we stand by the AV which reads 'propitiate', which means to appease one who is angry.

(I should say here that there is no perfect translation of the Scriptures: we turned some time ago from the AV in public reading to the RSV because the newer version involved us in less explanatory and paraphrastic comments, but it still has to be checked.)

Turn to 1 John 2:2, where practically the same Greek word for 'propitiation' in the AV is also translated 'expiation'. Again in 1 John 4:10: 'expiation' for our sins. They have changed the translation in these places, because, they say, this must refer to the removal of sin without reference to an angry God. We can't have an angry God. The God and Father of our Lord Jesus Christ can't be angry; it savours too much of superstition, heathenism, paganism. Well that, it seems to me, is like saying we must put out a fire without reference to the cause of the fire – such as fire-raisers or incendiary bombs. Nothing started it!

That is to say, the expiation of sin – not the propitiation of an angry God – is something done in a vacuum. It impersonalises the whole action. It is said that it is just a fact that we are sinners and have sinned, and by the redeeming work of Jesus Christ on the cross, sin is put away. It is 'expiated', without reference to God; not that God is excluded altogether, they could hardly do that, although some would go even as far as that, but they exclude any reference to a God who is angry with sinners. I hope you see that this is nonsense. Some have gone to great lengths; they have ransacked the Old Testament and the New Testament, and ransacked pagan literature, Greek and so on, to try to prove that this is so, because they do not like the idea of an angry God.

Now it must be quite clear, and it is to anyone who has sense (it is amazing how little sense some people have!), that the wrath of God spoken of in Romans 1:18 is holy wrath. It is the wrath of a holy God. And I want you to note in that connection that in 3:25 it is God who puts forward Jesus Christ as our propitiation. We don't offer to God our propitiation.

Another of their objections to the idea of an angry God being appeased, is that the pagans offer gifts to appease their gods when calamities come upon them. But we don't offer gifts to God to appease his anger; it is God Himself who provides the Gift we give back again to Him, Jesus Christ. It is He who puts forward His own Son, Christ crucified, to be our propitiation.

Note that it does not say that Christ is put forward to be our Propitiator, although He is. That is to say, He is not offered us merely as a Saviour who does something for us, but He is offered us as Someone who, having done something for us, is Himself the Propitiation. It is Christ who is our propitiation, not merely what He has done – although, of course, it is Christ having wrought efficaciously, that is offered to us: but it is not the mere fruit, as if Christ handed you something and said, 'Here is your redemption; here is your forgiveness,' and then ran away; as a messenger hands a gift in at the door, and the door shuts and away goes the messenger; he has done his job. Not a bit of it! It is Christ Himself, the Worker, who comes to us Himself. It is Christ, personally, who is our salvation, because we become new creatures in Him; and it is Christ Himself, personally, who comes to us with all the efficacy, the fruit of what He has done, and is the propitiation for our sin.

'Yes,' you say, 'you keep using that long word, and some of us don't know what it means.' Well one way of translating the word 'propitiation', which should possibly be found in the RSV of Romans 3:25 and elsewhere, is simply to call it by the term, 'mercy-seat'. If you looked at Hebrews 9:5 you would find the word 'mercy-seat' there, and it is exactly the same word in the Greek here. I'm not saying it should be translated the same, but it is exactly the same word in the Greek, and it is there translated, 'mercy-seat'.

You want to know what propitiation means? Let

me take you back to the Jewish Tabernacle in the wilderness. God gave Israel the dimensions and prescribed the furnishings of the place in which they were to worship God; with its outer court, and brazen altar on which they sacrificed the animals, and the laver for washing themselves before they entered the first division of the Tabernacle. Within that, the Holy Place, were three pieces of furniture: the table of the shewbread, the seven-branched candlestick, the altar of incense; all of gold. Then there was the curtain, and behind it the ark of the covenant, the wooden chest completely overlaid with gold, so that no wood was to be seen. Inside the chest were the two tables of the Ten Commandments, the Decalogue as we call it (see Ex. 20 and Deut. 5). As the Ark stands hidden in that unspeakably dark inner chamber called the Holy of Holies, there is a seat on top of the ark, overlaid with purest gold. Who sits there? God sits there. That is His Judgment Seat, and He is judging men according to the Ten Commandments inscribed on the tables within the chest. That is the Judgment Seat.

Then, one day in the year only, in the month of October, on the Day of Atonement, the High Priest of Israel will dare to part the curtain and go into that place where no one is to enter on any day of the year – except this one man only. If any other man entered he would be smitten to death. But the High Priest does not enter empty-handed; he enters with a vessel bearing the blood of the animal which has been sacrificed outside, and very fearfully he takes of the blood in the basin and sprinkles it on the golden seat above the Ten Commandments. It is the blood of the Lamb. God is there: invisibly, we may think of Him, but that is His seat.

But it is then no longer a Judgment Seat, but a Mercy Seat. The sins of the people not only have been expiated, blotted out by the sacrifice of the Lamb, who, of course, is the Lord Jesus Christ, but the anger of God, who is seated on the Judgment Seat, and who is wrathful with men because they have broken His commandments – every one of them – is appeased, assuaged, exhausted, and it is then mercy, not judgment, which He dispenses from that seat to those who will come to Him by the blood of the Lamb.

That is what propitiation means, and you can see it when it is applied to the Lord Jesus Christ in His death on the cross for us. For our text, 'The wrath of God is revealed from heaven', tells us that God is angry with sinners in their sins. I said to you a moment ago that you find the wrath of God expressed in many places in the Old Testament and in the New, perhaps more often in the New than in the Old. For it is our Lord Himself at this point who says, 'He who believes in the Son has eternal life; he who does not obey the Son, shall not see life, but the wrath of God rests on him' (John 3:36).

We find the wrath of God mentioned quite a number of times in the Book of the Revelation, more often there than anywhere else; and we even read in 6:16, 17, of 'the wrath of the Lamb'. Not only is

God, who sits on that Judgment Seat, angry with sinners, but the Lamb Himself, who spilt His blood for the forgiveness of sins and the deliverance of sinners, is angry with men because of their rejection of His sacrifice and the atonement He has made.

Back again to our text: 'The wrath of God is revealed from heaven against all ungodliness and unrighteousness of men.' If you were to scan the first chapter of Romans from verse 18 onwards, you would see that God is angry with men because they turn their backs on Him so that they may not feel the guilt of their wicked deeds. He is angry with them because of their sins, but He is much more angry with them because they won't face their sins, admit them and turn to God to receive forgiveness for them. They turn their backs upon Him, because they cannot stand the feelings of guilt and shame which come over them when they know they commit wicked deeds in God's sight. They ignore what they see of God in nature, blind their eyes to the glories of nature. (The sunset tonight! The glimpse that I had of the last remnants of the sunset – it was marvellous! Just a little strip of light, and etched against it, silhouetted against it, a few chimney pots. It was so beautiful against the dark of the night as I looked, that it spoke of the glories of God's creation and of His grace and goodness.)

But men turn their backs upon God as they see Him in nature; men turn their backs upon God as they know Him in their own consciences (that is the beginning of Romans 2). Men turn their backs upon

God as they see Him in the Commandments and in the whole Old Testament law. Men even turn their backs upon God – sometimes most of all – when they see Him in the holy Gospel, where both the grace of God and the wrath of God are revealed, because the anger of God is revealed in that cross. Rich blood was spilt because of men's sins, so there is wrath there, as well as mercy. There would have been no need of mercy if men had not sinned, and God was not wrathful with them.

Men turn their backs upon all the light God shines upon their paths, the glories of nature as God has created it (fallen as it now is), the light that God has streamed into men's consciences to know what is right and what is wrong, the light that God has given to men by His holy Law in the Old Testament and the far greater, blazing light in the Gospel. Men have turned their backs, and today are still turning their backs on all that. Why? Because they want to go on living their own lives and doing what they want and living in their sins; and since this is so, they dismiss the Christian church, they dismiss the Christian Gospel, they dismiss the Bible and they dismiss anything that has to do with good at all, simply because they want to live their own kind of lives.

We understand, of course, why this is. They are blinded, have shut their eyes and have turned away, all because they have been wrought upon by a certain character, a loathsome enemy of God, the devil. And that is why Paul, speaking about those who are blind, having turned their backs upon God, and who therefore cannot see the glory of His grace, says of them, 'In their case the god of this world has blinded the minds of the unbelievers' (2 Cor. 4:4). The devil has blinded men's minds. Indeed, when they turn against God they don't even know that they are being wrought upon. When men turn their backs on the Gospel, they think they are doing it all by their own intelligent wit and will. They don't like it. They don't believe it. 'Away with your Bible and your Gospel,' they say. But they don't know that they are being wrought upon by the devil, that it is he who makes them do it. But that is what the Gospel says, 'In their case the god of this world has blinded the minds of unbelievers.' None the less, they are responsible for yielding to the enemy and for following him, even although they do not know him as such, nor call him by his name. They still have consciences; that is why Paul, writing to the Ephesians and speaking about men who have turned their backs upon God and His holy Gospel, calls them 'children of wrath'. Of these he says, 'We (Jews) all once lived in the passions of our flesh, following the desires of body and mind, and so we were by nature children of wrath, like the rest of mankind (Gentiles)' (Eph. 2:3).

So men who turn their backs upon God are children of wrath, although they are unaware that God is angry with them. How can they know that God is angry with them? How can they see His flaming wrath when the devil has come to them and wrought upon them and they have gladly welcomed his attentions, until they are blinded to the truth, and then they themselves turn away in hate? They are absolutely unaware of it. If they really knew that God in heaven was flaming angry with them in their sins, they would not sin as they do. And they will not know until the Spirit of God breaks into their consciences and tells them, 'God is angry with you for what you do and what you are!'

That is exactly what happened to David when he took another man's wife and, to get her, murdered her husband. He committed adultery, and then murder. Now here was a man who had quite a lot of light, because God had regarded him as a very favoured person and had revealed very wonderful things to him; and yet, in a moment, because he was greatly tempted in his own passions, he turned his back upon God and lusted after that woman; and to get her, had her husband slain in the battle. But, because God doesn't wink at our sins but knows every sin we commit, He sent His prophet Nathan to him to say, 'David, I've a story to tell you.' And Nathan told him the story of the man who, having guests come to his home, instead of taking of his own large flock to make a feast for them, helped himself to the one ewe lamb of a poor man.

When David heard the story, he was furious with the man for taking the poor man's one ewe lamb to make a meal for his guests; but Nathan said to him, 'Wait a moment, David; not so angry, unless you are being so with yourself, because you are the man. That is what you have done. You have plenty wives, far too many, and this godly man Uriah, who was not even of your nation, had one lovely wife Bathsheba; and because you had not enough wives and concubines of your own, you have taken his one, lovely, pure wife and have killed her husband to get her. You do right to be angry at this story, David, if you are angry with yourself!'

It was thus that David knew what he had done. He did not know beforehand, or, rather, would not let himself know that God was angry with him for his sin. David never prospered after that. He might have laid down his head and died there and then, because there was no good in his life.

But you see the point? God had broken into the darkness of David's wicked heart and mind through the prophet, and had streamed light into his soul to show him how angry God was with his sin. Then – this is the interesting thing – David later wrote a poem about it, and in that poem he neither speaks of the wrong he did Uriah, the man he had murdered, nor the wrong he did his wife, committing adultery with her, nor the wrong he did himself, being God's servant and the king of Israel, nor the wrong he did Israel by leading them into trouble that lasted for generations and generations. He does not speak of the wrong he had done the man, or the woman, or himself, or anybody, but the wrong he had done God. He was so filled with the knowledge of what he had done in God's sight, the wicked, horrid and filthy thing he had done in God's sight, that this is what he says, 'Against thee, thee only, have I sinned, and done that which is evil in thy sight, so that thou art justified in thy sentence and blameless in thy judgment' (Psa. 51:4). O God, it is against You, it is against You only! That doesn't mean to say that he hadn't sinned against the man and the woman, and against himself, but it meant that the sin he had committed against God was so heinous that the sin he had sinned against the others seemed slight, almost, in his sight, compared with the fact that he had wronged his God who had blessed him so.

Do you see what that tells us? When the light streams into our souls and we realise that God is angry with us in our sins (the things we treat so lightly and joke about), the revelation fills all our horizon. The whole sky becomes black and we see nothing but the anger of God filling the whole universe and smothering our souls; so much so, that when it descends upon us as an unspeakable blackness, our sin seems so heinous in the light of God's wrath that it seems impossible for it ever to be forgiven. We believe, then, that there is no possibility of forgiveness, nothing in the world can ever atone for such an enormity of sin.

Yet, you see, we are so made, that we say, 'But I must try. O God, I must try to make amends. I must try to atone for my sin, God. You cannot forgive me. It would be indecent for You to forgive my sin. It would be dishonourable, it would be unjust; it would be a monstrous wrong for You to forgive my sin. God, You can't do it. I must atone. I must make amends. How will I make amends? Punish me, God. Visit me with Your wrath. Visit me with Your judgment. I must pay for my sin. If not, I will have to punish myself and suffer every day of my life until I have paid for my sin.'

That is what conviction of sin says, when we see the wrath of God for our sin. Then someone comes along with the Bible in his hand and says, 'Yes, you are a wicked fellow. God says so, and I agree with you that what you have done is very, very wicked. But look, the Gospel says that God forgives. He forgives sinners.' 'Oh, no,' you say, 'He can't; it's too cheap. He can't forgive my sin. Nothing that He could do, could forgive my sin. Only I myself can forgive my sin by atoning for it. I must pay for it by suffering. It's too cheap that He should forgive me.' Then the preacher, or the witness, with the Bible in his hand, begins to speak about the death of Jesus, and says, 'Do you know what this Book says? One day, God sent His Son for sinners. He put Him on that cross and thrashed Him to death for sinners. The sinless One, who never sinned one sin from birth to death, not one sin of thought or word or deed! God thrashed all the sins of all men on Him unto death. God vented all His wrath for the sins of men – including your sins – upon Him, so that you could go free and really be forgiven.'

That is not cheap; and the proof of it is that Christ in heaven, who is now the Advocate, is praying night and day (and there is no night there), praying for repentant and believing sinners, saying, 'O God, You must keep forgiving them, because remember, I died for them. You must forgive them, Father. I know they are bad and wayward and perverse, but You must forgive them, because I died for them.'

'So,' says the preacher, 'He died for you in particular. He was thrashed for your sins; the thrashing, the punishment, the judgment for what you did, if it was a sin like David's, or anyone else's, has been paid for. He was thrashed to death for it. There is nothing you can do and nothing you need do. It is done.'

Listen to this hymn by Augustus Montague Toplady; you know it well:

> Rock of Ages, cleft for me, (that is, Christ's death)
> Let me hide myself in Thee;
> Let the water and the blood,
> From Thy riven side which flowed,
> Be of sin the double cure,
> Cleanse me from its guilt and power.
>
> Not the labours of my hands
> Can fulfil Thy Law's demands;
> Could my zeal no respite know,
> Could my tears forever flow,
> All for sin could not atone:
> Thou must save and Thou alone.
>
> Nothing in my hand I bring,
> Simply to Thy Cross I cling;
> Naked, come to Thee for dress;
> Helpless, look to Thee for grace;
> Foul, I to the fountain fly;
> Wash me, Saviour, or I die.

Or this hymn by Charles Wesley:

Jesus, Lover of my soul,
Let me to Thy bosom fly,
While the nearer waters roll,
While the tempest still is high;
Hide me, O my Saviour, hide,
Till the storm of life is past;
Safe into the haven guide;
O receive my soul at last!

Other refuge have I none;
Hangs my helpless soul on Thee;
Leave, ah! leave me not alone;
Still support and comfort me.
All my trust on Thee is stayed;
All my help from Thee I bring;
Cover my defenceless head
With the shadow of Thy wing.

Thou, O Christ, art all I want;
More than all in Thee I find;
Raise the fallen, cheer the faint,
Heal the sick, and lead the blind.
Just and holy is Thy Name,
I am all unrighteousness;
False and full of sin I am,
Thou art full of truth and grace.

Plenteous grace with Thee is found
Grace to cover all my sin;
Let the healing streams abound;
Make and keep me pure within.
Thou of life the fountain art,
Freely let me take of Thee;
Spring Thou up within my heart,
Rise to all eternity.

This is the sin of sins, that when you have been convicted of your sin, when you know the wrath of God is upon you because you have sinned and someone comes to you with the Gospel, you say, 'Oh, no, I can't take that; it's too cheap!' The death of Jesus, too cheap! 'I must make atonement for my own sin.' That is the sin of sins, which will not let God forgive you, because you are so proud. You will not even forgive yourself, you are so proud; you will never forgive yourself for sinning when you learn what you did not know before, that God is angry with you.

This is the second shaft of light that has to stream into our souls. The first is a horrid shaft of light which reveals how angry God is with us. The second is far more difficult for us to accept. It is to know that God forgives us freely by the death of Jesus Christ, and all we have to do is to lift our hands (and He even helps us do that) to receive His salvation, His redemption. It is so humbling to accept His mercy. 'No, no,' we say. 'Justice! Justice! I will not accept justice vested in Another. I will only accept justice that has been done by myself. My pride will not allow me to accept this great sacrifice which Christ has made for me. I cannot accept. I will try to save myself.'

So, to come to Jesus Christ involves two deaths: the death of learning what wicked sinners we are in His sight and how angry God is with us; and the death to our pride; coming with empty hands like beggars and saying, 'Oh, God, I'm undone; I've made an awful mess of it and I can do nothing to undo it, but You have done something for me. I accept it. I accept Him, the propitiation concerning my sins. Come and forgive me. Come and forgive my sins and take me into Your heart, a saved sinner.' Will you?

> Depth of Mercy! can there be,
> Mercy still reserved for me?
> Can my God His wrath forbear?
> Me the chief of sinners, spare?

6

LIBERATION OF PERSONALITY
BY THE GOSPEL
Reading: 2 Corinthians 3

I want to speak about liberation of personality by the Gospel of Jesus Christ. I will touch on certain aspects of it, principally related to guilt and fear, but we can go on from there to deal with other aspects, if God guides that way. I want to begin by thinking of two enslaving elements, not unconnected, in the personality of Peter, the disciple.

First I want to look at his preoccupation with himself: even after three years in the Lord's company Peter was still a self-regarding, inturned personality, constantly taken up with himself. The cry of his heart was always, 'What about me? What about me? What about me?' We see it at Caesarea Philippi, after he had wonderfully confessed the Lord, and the Lord began to tell the disciples that He was going to Jerusalem to die. Peter was deeply concerned that Jesus should not die; because he truly loved Him, there was no question about that. But if Jesus was going to Jerusalem to die, what was going to happen to Peter? That was his chief concern. We see it on the Mount of Transfiguration. Peter, James and John were in the presence of something far too big for them, and poor Peter was overshadowed; the focus of attention was not on him, and he didn't like it.

Some people are like that; they can't stand company unless they are in the midst of it. They must be the focus. They can't be one of a crowd. It is a sickness, you know. Peter prattled; he just blethered. Scripture says so!

Then the feet washing (as I interpret the feet washing), when Jesus went round washing the disciples' dirty feet, Peter objected; he had to be different from the rest. He knew better than they how to behave. Again, at the end of the same chapter (John 13), the Lord indicated that in the fulness of time the disciples (many of them, at any rate) would follow Him, presumably to martyrdom – but not yet. 'But,' said Peter, 'why can't I follow you now, Lord?' You see?

And in Gethsemane – the sword. Was he afraid for his Master in the garden that he would be arrested? Yes, but he was afraid for himself, that is why he fled with the others. Was he afraid for his Lord? If he had been afraid for his Lord he would not have run away, he would have gone all the way to the cross with Him, and he didn't. Self, self, self! Oh, we needn't blame him, because we are all touched with that disease, and when we read about Peter, we are reading about ourselves. It is the occasions only which are different.

Do you remember when they went out to the lake to fish and they came back having had no success? Then the Lord sent them out again and they came back with their nets full of fish, and Peter said to the Lord, 'Depart from me, for I am a sinful man, O Lord' (Luke 5:8). Now notice what he said, 'Depart from me, for I am a sinful man, O Lord.' He was preoccupied with himself and with his sin and because he was preoccupied with that, he was really saying, 'O Lord, go away; I can't stand You so near. You make me feel so sinful. Go away.' Can you see the connection between the self and the sin? You see, the one reacts upon the other, the self-regard, the self-centredness and the sin, because our selfishness is convicted by God's holy Law, the Ten Commandments.

The first four commandments say, 'Worship God, first of all.' Then, the fifth, 'Care for your father and mother.' 'Do not steal.' 'Do not commit adultery', and so on ... 'Care for other people.' And we are guilty when we read such laws, because they strike home to our consciences, and when they do, we are condemned. Now, I want you to see the connection between God's holy Law, the Ten Commandments, and a sense of sin; for Paul says in Romans 3:20 that it is through the Law (the Ten Commandments, God's holy Law given to us to show us how to be good) that the knowledge of sin comes. God says, 'You must not do that,' and we are convicted of sin because we have done it.

In Romans 4:15 Paul says, 'The law brings wrath, but where there is no law there is no transgression.' You see, until God says, 'You mustn't do that,' you may be at fault, but you haven't sinned. You may have committed a crime, but in the strict sense you haven't sinned, because you did not have the knowledge of sin, which only comes when the Law says, 'Thou shalt not.' Listen to these three verses, and see how much you can take from them: 'Therefore,' says Paul, 'as sin came into the world through one man and death through sin, and so death spread to all men because all men sinned....' Then he breaks off and says, 'Sin indeed was in the world before the law was given, but sin is not counted where there is no law. Yet death reigned from Adam to Moses....' (Romans 5:12-14a).

One other place towards the end of that chapter (5:20, 21): Paul says, 'The law came in' with Moses. Men sinned in Adam (a long time before Moses), but the Law only came with Moses. It was only when God gave Moses the Ten Commandments and he came down the mountain with the two tablets, that sin, in a sense, was revealed to the world, because God then said in His holy Law, 'Thou shalt not.' And men were convicted of their sin. 'The law came in,' says Paul, 'to increase the trespass (to make it appear very bad, as we read in another chapter); but where sin increased, grace abounded all the more, so that, as sin reigned in death, grace also might reign through righteousness to eternal life through Jesus Christ our Lord.'

It all goes back to the vicious circle which began with the Fall, when Adam and Eve first fell into sin. It was then that human nature was entangled in sin and almost strangled in its entanglement; certainly it was all tied up. Then God gave His holy Law to men to say , 'Here, you! You can't do that; that is against my Law. Read, and see that you can't do that!' And then men became convicted of sin.

But something else happened. When God said, 'Thou shalt not!' when He placarded the world with His Law, 'You can't do that' men said (because they were fallen creatures, of course), 'Who said I can't do that? I will do that.' And the perversity, the latent perversity which was in Adam from the time that he rebelled against God and chose to go Satan's way, rose like a great gorge, and he said, 'I will.' 'Keep off the grass? Not likely! I'll tramp on the grass.'

So, you see, God's Law, His holy 'Thou shalt not,' not only reveals sin to men – (Are you following? You must follow this, for it is important.) – it not only reveals what sinners men are, but it puts the devil into them, and makes them sin the more. Now notice this, it is God's holy, perfect Law which incites men to sin, not because there is anything wrong with it, but because man, being sinful before the Law came, is incited to fresh sin, perversity and rebellion, when the Law says, 'You must not do that.' This comes from Satan: this is the depths of the enmity in the heart of the devil against God and against God's men.

The devil uses absolutely everything he can to do despite to God, and he knows he can spite God most by spiting Him in His creature, man; for man is God's prize exhibit. He is far prouder of men than He is of angels, or beasts, or trees. When the devil enslaved man, Adam, the crown of God's creation, this was the worst he could do against God. And when God sent His holy Law to say to men, 'You can't do that; You mustn't do that,' the devil said, 'I'll see that they do. I'll make them want to do it all the more. This is the very thing I wanted. Hurrah for the Law! I'll put my own Satanic power into them. I'll make them mad at the Law and they'll sin more and more'; because as Paul says in the great resurrection chapter (1 Cor. 15:56), 'The strength of sin is the Law,' and God's Law is good, not bad. 'The strength of sin is the Law.'

As a climax to all this, take these words and never forget them: 'The strength' – this is something for thinking people to ponder this week to come: 'The strength of sin is the Law' – and God's Law is good. What is bad, then? It is the devil who is bad, and sin within us, because they use God's holy Law to incite us to greater sin.

But then the Gospel says that in Christ, when Christ has come to take us into Himself, to give Himself to us, in Christ, we are not under the Law any longer; we are under grace. We are no longer within the sphere of the Law when we are converted, when we receive Jesus Christ, when we become Christians, when we are born again, when we are saved – use any language you like. We are transferred from the kingdom of darkness to the kingdom of light. We become different creatures. No, we may not look different, not outwardly, at any rate, to begin with, but we become different creatures, because we now belong to another world. We are within the kingdom of grace and not that of law.

That is exactly what Paul is saying in the first four verses of Romans 7. I want to make them as clear as I can. Paul is saying that as sinners we are bound by the Law to this Adam, but then Christ has come to slay Adam, the fallen, perverse Adam in you and in me. Christ has come to slay him. And Paul says, 'Now we are free from him to be joined to another.' He uses a marriage metaphor. The Christian is like a woman bound to a bad husband. He is Adam. He is a rebel, a rotter. She is bound to him by law, she is married to him; but Jesus comes to slay the rotter, Adam. She is therefore not bound by the law of that marriage any longer, because he is dead, and she is free to marry another; and the other is Christ.

In summing up these four verses, Paul says, 'Likewise, my brothers, you have died to the law through the body of Christ, so that you may belong to another.' Now, when you read difficult passages, don't try necessarily to understand every word. Don't stick at a bit, and say, 'I can't go on until I understand what it all means.' Run over it again and again, backwards and forwards, to see if a few words, a phrase in it, gives you light, then read it again and perhaps you will have more light. 'Likewise, my brothers, you have died to the law through the body of Christ, so that you may belong to another, to him who has been raised from the dead in order that we may bear fruit for God. While we were living in the flesh (Adam), our sinful passions, aroused by the law, were at work in our members to bear fruit for death. But now we are discharged from the law, dead to that which held us captive, so that we serve not under the old written code but in the new life of the Spirit' (Romans 7:4-6).

We are delivered from the Law. We are delivered from its paralysing demand, because Christ, in a sense, takes down the placard with the Law. He doesn't destroy it, because it is holy; it is never destroyed; it is holy. He came to fulfil it; but He takes it down and puts it away. He delivers us from its paralysing demand. He delivers us from its guilt, its accusing finger. He delivers us from its incitement to sin, which raises our ire when we see it; and He puts Himself in its place and smiles at us and says, 'Look, you will never be good by following that finger pointing to the Law, but look at Me smiling at you, loving you, caring for you, forgiving you. I will save you.' This is what a great many professing Christians will not take in. Yes, professing Christians, this is what we're talking about! Christ takes down the Law with its paralysing demand, its condemnation and its incitement to sin, and sets Himself up in its stead: He is the Master of the Law. He is the Giver of the Law. He has fulfilled the Law, by living a perfect, human life on earth for thirty-three years.

He fulfilled the Law a second way, by bearing its punishment for us. So He has a right to take it down. If any one can take it down, He can. If any one says, 'You can't take that down; that is good,' He says, 'I can take it down. I gave it. I'm the Master of it. I gave it in the first place, to Moses, through the angels. I fulfilled it, living according to it as no man on earth has ever done, for thirty-three years, and then bore the punishment for the sins of those who hadn't fulfilled it; and if any man has a right to take it down (I'm not going to destroy it), I have.' And He takes it down.

It is quite wrong for us Christians to live under the Law, to be bowed down with a sense of guilt, and to be taken up, all the time, with sin and the Law. That is legal, and many young Christians today are living legal lives. They say their prayers, perform their devotions and do their service for Christ in a legal fashion, wondering every moment whether He will come down on them with His chopper and smite them if they don't do it exactly right. This is warping and spoiling a great many young lives, and I'm more deeply concerned about it than I can say. In Christ we are under grace, and we have to learn to put the Law aside – no, we are not destroying it, but we must put it aside, because we have something better than God's holy Law; we have God Himself, in Christ. Look at Christ, He alone can deliver us from the condemnation of the Law.

I intended to wade through much of Romans 6 this evening, but I'm not going to do it. We'll look at two verses at the beginning of Romans 8. Paul says, 'There is therefore now no condemnation for those who are in Christ Jesus' (8:1). Then he introduces another law, not Moses' law, but another law or principle. He says, 'For the law (or principle) of the Spirit of life in Christ Jesus has set me free from the law of sin and death' (8:2). So there is no more looking to the Law, but looking to Christ. It is not by looking to God's holy Law that we'll be changed. It is not by looking to God's holy Law that we will find the liberty and joy and satisfaction we want and need; that is not the way. Even when we have sinned – careful now, careful! – even when we have sinned, what do we do then? Usually, like Peter, we run from Christ saying, 'Goodbye, Lord. I can't come near You, I have sinned. I'm a sinner. I can't come near You.' But the Lord says, 'Man, you're under grace, not under Law. I know you have sinned and I hate sin, but I don't hate you and I'll accept your sin and deal with it because I love you. You are more important to me than sin, whether you do it or don't do it.'

Now I told you to be careful. Some people could twist this round and go out to say I had uttered the most dreadfully blasphemous and heretical words here tonight, but that is not true. Under the sphere of grace, when we sin – God doesn't put a premium on sin. He doesn't subsidise sin, how could He? He hates it – but under the sphere of grace, when we sin, He forgives it. 'If we walk in the light, as he is in the light, we have fellowship with one another, and the blood of Jesus his Son keeps cleansing us from all sin. If we say we have no sin, we deceive ourselves, and the truth is not in us. If we confess our sins, he is faithful and just, and will forgive our sins and cleanse us from all unrighteousness' (1 John 1:7-9).

Then in 1 John 2:1 he says, 'My little children....' Now a judge doesn't stand before train robbers and traitors and some of the horrid murderers that stand before judges nowadays, and say to them sweetly, 'My little children!' But this is what Jesus says to sinning Christians. This is love. 'My little children, I am writing this to you so that you may not sin; but if any one does sin, we have an advocate with the Father (One to speak to God for us and plead His blood), Jesus Christ the righteous one.' He is an Advocate you can trust and He is the propitiation – this is what we were talking about last Sunday evening – He has borne the wrath and punishment of God for our sins; and not for ours only but also for the sins of the whole world. This is what is given us.

Of course, we have to keep short accounts with God. As soon as we know we have sinned, we must run to Him – not run away from Him like Peter and say, 'Depart from me, O Lord, I have sinned.' Do you see how wrong we all are in this? We are to run to Him and say, 'O Lord, I have sinned.' Children may run from their parents when they have done wrong, but, Christianwise, my friends, that isn't right. Run to Him.

But then – let me try to sum this up – Satan's major strategy in our lives is to plug the Law, plug the Law, plug the Law; all that is negative, all that is condemnatory, to bring us into bondage to the Law. Guilt, guilt, guilt! You have sinned, run away from God, He hates you. You rascal, you have sinned. You are hopeless! It is the devil who is saying that, not God. You may not believe it, but it is the devil. We are under grace.

I'm speaking about this because there are influences amongst Christian young people today which are dangerous, and I'm going to fight them to the death, wherever they come from. A holy gorge has risen in my soul against false teaching, and some of you young Christians – and I'm warning you now – are weighed down with false, lugubrious, paralysing teaching about the Word, and it is making you more and more guilty, more and more afraid. You are regarding God more and more as a kind of policeman, always wagging His finger at you about your sin and your wordliness and all the bad things you are and do. And it is making some of you glum, sad, self-preoccupied, over-serious, falsely serious. It is stultifying and inhibiting you. With others, it is having the reverse effect of making them far more frivolous than they want to be, because they feel they've got to escape from the awful sense of sin.

This is not honouring to God who spilt the blood of His dear Son to bring you under grace, forgiveness and love. It is love – let me say it again, I hope I will say it thousands of times before the breath goes out of my body – it is only love that saves. Law will never save a soul. We are not honouring the gracious work of Christ when we are living according to the Law. This leads to all the guilt complexes that so many have today, young and not so young, by which we feel it is our duty to thrash ourselves. We think it is a virtue – in private of course: we don't let the world know we are doing this. We think it a virtue constantly to castigate ourselves.

Have you read any of David Brainerd? I remember a young man who was here for years and is now in the ministry, becoming sadder and sadder, until one day I said to him, 'What in the world is ado with you?' 'Oh, Mr. Still, have you read David Brainerd?' 'Oh, yes, I have, a little; but I'll read him a bit more, if you think it would be good for me!' Of course, David Brainerd was a wonderful man and there were wonderful things done in his day; he saw revival amongst the Red Indians. But the writings of his own private meditations are so full of preoccupation with sin that in the end I got quite sick of it and said to my young friend, 'I know now why you get sadder and sadder, my boy. You are under an unhealthy influence. David Brainerd, or no David Brainerd, you give up that book.'

Thrashing, you see. Do you know the word 'masochistic'? Do you know what masochism is? It is taking pleasure in thrashing yourself. Do you know there are queer, perverted people who go around with a belt, or whip, or rod, inviting others to thrash them, because it gives them perverse pleasure; base, horrid pleasure? There are also people, perhaps the same people, who, having found a fiendish, devilish satisfaction in being thrashed until their bodies bleed, will take the belt or whip and do it to somebody else. They are sadists. People like that are sick, and though, I suppose, there is nobody as bad as that here – although one never knows who is sitting in the kirk – there are too many Christians who, spiritually speaking, are too far along that line. They have begun to be sick with a preoccupation with sin – muck!

I wanted to put on the textboard outside the church, but I could not get the right wording – it is very difficult to get something with few-enough words to be clear and bold enough to see as you pass by – I wanted to put something about stars and mud.

> Two men looked out of prison bars:
> One saw mud and the other stars.

It is mud, muck; raking amongst the muck! That will never save you.

The question arises: Do people who are sick and are preoccupied with sin, guilt, the Law and all that sort of thing, do they look for a sick theology or doctrine in the Bible and in other writings because they are sick, or does this kind of teaching make them sick? Which is first? I don't know. I think some are sick, and then find this kind of teaching in great old-fashioned tomes, and feed on it, like poison to their souls, like anti-Christian bad news; not the Gospel, which is good news. Some are sick before and this makes them more sick. Some are not sick, but they are drawn in by the influence of friends.

I warn you, 'Be careful!' I don't care who you are influenced by, be careful you are not drawn in by the influence of friends to read and read and read until you become sick like them. I want to say this: people who dispense this kind of thing are often very good advertisements for it, because they themselves are unliberated personalities: if you see some one going around with this, offering you this as if it were the only doctrine that is really worth, you should say to him or her, 'Well, give us a smile first, and then we'll have a look!' It's a vicious circle, you see; a spiral that goes down, down, down into a vortex, until we are sucked into manifest unhealth.

I want to speak very plainly, for some of you have been under this negative, this beating-of-the-breast, this thrashing theology, too much within the last year or two, and some have been so belaboured by it and threatened into it that you are punch-drunk with allegedly holy blows, until you scarcely know, Christianwise, who you are or where you are going. My advice to you is that whoever has influenced you, however intellectual, or intelligent or well-read he may be, you must shake him off! There are whole libraries of this kind of thing, by which many obsessed devotees interpret the Bible – far less healthy than the Bible – and I am fighting this influence all the time, because it is dangerous. Shake it off. Refuse it, and its gloomy advocates. Why, even the so-called gloomy prophet Jeremiah could teach you better than that. Read for yourselves Jeremiah chapter 29, and particularly verses 1-14.

That's the weeping prophet, but he isn't weeping there, and he isn't weeping here: listen to this: 'I will set my eyes upon them for good, and I will bring them back to this land. I will build them up, and not tear them down; I will plant them, and not uproot them. I will give them a heart to know that I am the LORD; and they shall be my people and I will be their God, for they shall return to me with their whole heart' (Jer. 24:6-7).

That is the so-called weeping prophet. You see how positive, constructive, happy and optimistic he is. It was God who made him that, because our God is a happy God. And if you think that your God, your Jesus has made you glum and miserable, then you have got hold of the wrong god; you are in league with the devil, whether you know it or not. God wants us to be happy, holily happy, of course.

Now some of you, perhaps by your upbringing and training, or by the influences you have been under, deeply distrust happiness, and you are sure that it has a sinful cause. I believe there are some when they hear me talking like this (and I have been talking like this for quite some time now and it is not influencing some as I want them to be influenced), I believe that some of you suspect that I am speaking from sin. How wrong you are. I've shown you from the Bible that you are wrong: read what you like.

There is another side to it. There are sorrows, and there are tears, and there are wrestlings with the devil before God, and a whole lot more; but wasn't it Jesus who said, 'Do your weeping in private. Come out to the world with a smiling face.' Don't let it be a grin; let it come from a heart which is truly happy. Yes, there are struggles, yes, there are tears, yes, there are sorrows; but there is happiness, none the less. It is God who makes us happy. No one else can make us really happy deep down, for it is by yielding the whole life to Him who is the Spirit of liberty, the true, holy, purposive Spirit of freedom and liberty that we are happy.

This is what Peter found at Pentecost. You need only look at Peter after Pentecost: what a different man he was. Mind you, he was still a bit impulsive and emotional. Look at Peter in the first chapter of the Acts of the Apostles; then look at the apostle Paul towards the end of the Acts, then read him in all his letters. They are two different characters. Paul, in a sense, was a much more stable character, yet he had, none the less, freedom and liberty.

Take three men. First, Peter. Peter was by nature, temperamentally, an excitable, impulsive sort of chap. When the Holy Spirit came to him, he could scarcely contain; and he would almost dance. Now Paul wasn't like that; he was an intellectual, yet he was still free. He didn't gesticulate; he didn't go like some people you know! But he was, none the less, free. Then take Jesus. He is far more balanced and controlled than Paul or Peter, perfectly so; but the reason for that is that He had no sin to get rid of.

Christ came and had that perfect liberty which was seen in a gracious poise, which was, nevertheless, free; far freer than Peter and some people with their antics. Some people can't help antics when they are set free, that is the way they are made; some not so much; but the important thing is that whether we dance or smile, we are free. That is what some folk are not.

'All hail!' said Jesus after the resurrection. Oh, what a greeting that was! I think they change it in some of the modern translations, but let us keep that one; I like it, it is so full-blooded. 'All hail!' He said to them. Now that was as near to dancing, I think, as the perfectly balanced Lord of Life and Glory ever came. 'All hail!' He said.

Does your cheerless theology forbid an 'All hail'? Some are so sick with a humourless, joyless, dejected, despairing, oppressed, wretched, doleful, despondent death-wish, that they couldn't for the life of them face a resurrection. Some want to live at Gethsemane and Calvary forever. Now be careful; we must, in a sense, live there, for that is the heart of our faith; but they want to live at Gethsemane and Calvary in a way that never gets through to the Resurrection – and joy. Never a resurrection, never an empty tomb, never an 'All hail!'

Come on, now. Some have to be converted tonight. I am speaking to Christians largely, although others who are not yet Christians may be listening. I am speaking to Christians. You have to be converted tonight. Do you know what I would like to do with some of you? I would like, if it were possible, to clear the pews and have a holy dance! Oh, shake off your shackles!

'Ah,' the lugubrious ones say, 'be careful of that man, and what he is teaching.' Let me say this: Who takes down the Law? Jesus can save you better than the Law. The Law cannot save you at all. He can, and does with a smile! Friends, this is service with a smile! Don't be so sick that you cannot take it. Let's have a Resurrection tonight; your resurrection, in Christ.

7

JESUS AND THE WOMAN
TAKEN IN ADULTERY
Reading: John 7:37 – 8:11

I hope those of you who were here last week will remember what we were talking about: it is imprinted vividly on my mind. I was speaking on the same subject in another place on Friday, and for me the whole thing was gathered into this: I remembered picturing for you the placard of the Ten Commandments which Moses had set up to convict men of their sins, and all that followed from that; and of Jesus coming and taking down the placard and putting it away – not to destroy it; He came to fulfil it, but not that way.

The Law had been given that they might live by it, not die; but none kept it that they might live. So Jesus came, saying, 'You'll never live, you'll never be saved, you'll never be Christians, you'll never get to heaven by looking at that; it will just break your hearts, good and true as it is. So I take it down. Look at Me. I'll save you, and I'll save you by your looking at Me.' More is involved than that, of course, but that is the essence of it, 'Look at Me; and whereas these Ten Commandments frowned at you because you had broken them all, I am smiling at you. I'm not smiling at your sins, but you are more important to Me than your sins, and I have come to forgive you your sins, that is, to remove them and cleanse you from them; if you look at Me and see Me smiling at you, then that is the way to become a Christian, and grow in Christian grace to maturity.'

That is what Paul means in his Roman letter when he says we are not under the Law, good and perfect Law as it is. (It was Christ who gave it and it is the sum of His character and the sum of His Father's character. If you want a transcript of the being and the character of God, look at the Ten Commandments.) 'You are not under law but under grace' (Rom. 6:14). And it is grace, God's love smiling down at us, which is going to save us as nothing else in the world will do.

Then Paul proceeds to tell this story (Rom. 7:1-3): 'Do you not know, brethren – for I am speaking to those who know the law – that the law is binding on a person only during his life? Thus a married woman is bound by law to her husband as long as he lives.' Before I continue, let it be said that the 'married woman' here, stands for our essential being, the Adam whom God created before he sinned, when he was perfect. 'Thus a married woman is bound by law to her husband....' The husband is fallen Adam to whom she joined herself through the Fall. 'Thus a married woman is bound by the law (of Moses) to her husband as long as he lives; but if her husband dies (and, of course, Christ slew Adam on the cross. He took Adam on Himself, and became the second Adam to slay him in Himself) she is discharged from the law concerning the husband.

Accordingly, she will be called an adulteress if she lives with another man while her husband is alive. But if her husband dies she is free from that law, and if she marries another man (and the other is Christ) she is not an adulteress.'

What he is saying is this: that we have been joined to fallen Adam through sin, but Christ came to deal with sin and fallen Adam. He came to slay him because there was nothing else to do with him. He was unsavable, because he belonged to the devil, was indeed a child of the devil; so Christ came to slay him that He might join us in our essential being to another husband, even Christ. So we are free from the Law that dominates us as fallen creatures, free from its condemnation and guilt and the incitement to sin that comes through it.

Paul goes on to say (7:4): 'Likewise, my brethren, you have died to the law through the body of Christ, so that you may belong to another, to him who has been raised from the dead in order that we may bear fruit for God.' Then he says: 'While we were living in the flesh....' But you say, 'Aren't we living in the flesh now?' Not the sinful flesh, not the fallen nature of Adam, if we are Christians. In fact, if you look at Romans 8:9 you will see that Paul says there, 'But you are not in the flesh, you are in the Spirit, if the Spirit of God really dwells in you.' You do see what he means by the flesh? It is not this 'stuff'. We are in that, right enough, or we wouldn't be here; but it is the fallen nature of Adam that he means here by the flesh.

Romans 7:5, 6: 'While we were living in the flesh, our sinful passions, aroused by the law....' Satan and sin, you see, inciting us against the law, putting the devil into us when we see that the Law says, 'Thou shalt not do this.' The devil stirs sin within us and says, 'You will do it: you'll resist, you'll rebel, you'll revolt against God placarding us with His Law!' 'While we were living in the flesh, our sinful passions, aroused by the law, were at work in our members to bear fruit for death (that is, condemning us to death – death here means condemnation). But now we are discharged from the law (as it condemns us), dead to that which held us captive, so that we serve not under the old written code but in the new life of the Spirit.'

The chapter we read last Sunday evening said the same. 'God ... has qualified us to be ministers of a new covenant, not in a written code but in the Spirit; for the written code kills (good as it is, perfect as it is), but the Spirit gives life' (2 Cor. 3:6).

But I'm sure there are young Christians here who are still puzzled about how we can really live a Christian life by looking at Christ smiling upon us. Well, there is no other way to live the Christian life. If you think you are going to live a better Christian life by taking your eyes off Him and working hard at being pure, honest, clean and true, you have another 'think' coming, for that is not the way; that gets you deeper and deeper into the mire. That is what Paul describes as happening to men in Romans chapter 1: they took their eyes off God and sank deeper and deeper into vileness and depravity. It is by looking at Christ smiling upon us in His grace, His saving grace, that alone we can be saved.

Paul recognises the struggles which go on in the breasts of Christians. I want to read this passage, if you will be patient with me. I'm coming to 'The Woman taken in Adultery' later on, but this is an introduction, and I'm linking what I said last week with what I want to say now. Listen carefully while I go over the passage in which Paul describes the struggles which some have, in fact all of us have, if we admit it.

He begins by arguing about the two 'I's' within him, the old carnal 'I', the Adam that Christ has slain, and the new 'I', the Christian 'I' which has been brought into our lives by the Holy Spirit. Romans 7:14-20: 'We know that the law is spiritual; but I am carnal, sold under sin. I do not understand my own actions. For I do not do what I want, but I do the very thing I hate. Now if I do what I do not want, I agree that the law is good. So then it is no longer I that do it, but sin which dwells within me. For I know that nothing good dwells within me, that is, in my (fallen) flesh. I can will what is right, but I cannot do it. For I do not do the good I want, but the evil I do not want is what I do. Now if I do what I do not want, it is no longer I that do it, but sin which dwells within me.' He is not excusing himself; he is stating a fact about the struggle within.

Then he goes on to say (Rom. 7:21-23): 'So I find it to be a law (or principle) that when I want to

133

do right, evil lies close at hand.' (I always put a 'D' before that word 'evil', there). 'When I want to do right, evil lies close at hand. For I delight in the law of God, in my inmost self, but I see in my members another law at war with the law of my mind and making me captive to the law of sin which dwells in my members.' Then he cries out, 'Wretched man that I am! Who will deliver me from this body of death?' By staring at the Law and saying, I will keep you? Never, never, never! Thanks be to God for deliverance through Jesus Christ our Lord – by looking to Him as the Israelites looked at the brazen serpent in the wilderness and were healed and saved.

Almost in the next breath, at the beginning of Romans 8, he says, 'There is therefore now no condemnation for those who are in Christ Jesus. For the law (or principle) of the Spirit of life in Christ Jesus has set me free from the law of sin and death.' There is therefore now no condemnation for those who are in Christ Jesus! (If you have the AV, you will see that there is added, 'Who walk not according to the flesh but according to the Spirit', but that does not belong there; it really belongs to the fourth verse and you read it there). 'There is therefore now no condemnation for those who are in Christ Jesus.' Full stop: a complete statement!

Condemnation is not the way to save people. The way to change people into good people is not by thrashing them all the time, but by drowning them in love – if you like to put it that way. There is no other way; it is only love that saves. 'Ah,' but you say, 'that sounds too easy.' No, it isn't easy. We may sin many times, and we do – but within the sphere of God's love, Jesus Christ's grace. There is no condemnation when Christians trip and fall and stumble and come down: there is forgiveness. There is forgiveness within accepted love: the love that accepts us without condemnation because Jesus died, is the love that forgives us our sins when we fall.

Listen to this: 'But if we walk in the light, as he is in the light, we have fellowship with one another, and the blood of Jesus his Son cleanses us from all sin. If we say we have no sin, we deceive ourselves, and the truth is not in us. If we confess our sins, he is faithful and just, and will forgive our sins and cleanse us from all unrighteousness.... My little children, I am writing this to you so that you may not sin; but if any one does sin (provision within the gracious, saving, forgiving, expansive, holy love of God for those who sin), we have an advocate with the Father, Jesus Christ the righteous; and he is the propitiation for our sins, and not for ours only but also for the sins of the whole world' (1 John 1:7-9; 2:1, 2).

Now in the light of all this – and I'm not sure how many of you have seen it or see through it – the grace which alone saves man is in Jesus Christ. If you have seen it, let us go on to 'The Woman taken in Adultery'.

Look at her. The first thing to notice is that she is a daughter of the Covenant, a Jewess, born within the Covenant, a daughter of Abraham. She is counted within the Covenant as a child of God, else the Judaic law would not apply to her, but it obviously did, as the context makes clear. So if you like, Jesus is dealing with a woman within the Covenant. 'The Law says,' said the men who brought her in, 'the Law says that she must be stoned to death.' They didn't expect Jesus to do it, though, or to say that they should do it. Oh no; they sensed His mercy, and that is what they didn't like about Him, He was too merciful.

But there was more to it than that. They hated Him, absolutely hated Him. The Law said that she should be stoned to death and the Jews were required to judge according to the Law. If they had been faithful, they would have judged according to the Law. If the Law was to be honoured and penalties were to be exacted, then she should be stoned to death, that was what the Law said. All right then, let this sinless Giver of the Law do it. 'You do it, Jesus, You are the sinless One. You gave the Law, You made it. You stone her to death.' 'No,' He said, 'if any of you are sinless and would like to do it, go ahead.' None of them was sinless! 'All right then,' said Jesus, 'the sinless One chooses not to do so, because He came to save and not to destroy.' Then He bent down and wrote on the ground (and no one will ever know what He wrote because He wrote on the ground and not on paper or papyrus or tablet); and then He stood up and they all went away. When they had all gone, He said to the woman, 'Where are your accusers? Has no one condemned you?'

You are free from condemnation. As far as the Law is concerned you can go.

Now He wasn't sending her away, really. He was saying to her, 'Woman, you are forgiven. You are now in a state of having been forgiven by Me, the only Man who has authority to forgive sins. And being now in a state of having been forgiven your sins, which is going to last forever, you are to live all your mortal life, and hereafter in glory, in the light of this smile that you see on My face, in the light of My grace. You are now to live a new life, because you have seen Me and I do not condemn you, but forgive you your sins – all of them. Your sins, which are many, are all blotted out. You are to live a new life in My love, because I want you to learn what love means, and when you learn what love means, you will be saved into purity, honesty, humility and charity, into grace. All this, all the Law that I take down, is to be fulfilled in your life, under the smile of My grace and for love's sake. And, fulfilling that Law by looking at the face of grace, you will know the wonder of forgiving love. This is the Law, the fulfilling of God's holy Law, this is the law or principle within forgiving love, within perpetual forgiving love.'

1 John 2:1 (AV): 'These things write I unto you, that ye sin not. And if any man sin, we have an advocate.' And His hours are twenty-four hours a day! You can go to Him, you can ring Him up by prayer at any hour of day or night, and say to Him, 'Lord Jesus Christ, look what I've done!' He will

say, 'I'll speak to the Father for you and I'll plead My wounds and My blood and He will forgive you and take you back again into His heart. You have never really been out of it and you never will be, but all estrangement and all disappointment, all that keeps you apart, all that hinders your blessing and the usefulness of your Christian life, will be absolutely removed and it will be as if it had never been.'

He will do that, seventy million times seven, if necessary, not because He likes you to go on sinning, but because you are His child and He could never put you out. You may be estranged from Him, as the Jews were estranged from God in Babylon for their sins; but He took them back again and He will take you back again into His heart of love and bless you as He blessed you before.

This is the Law that operates within forgiving love. Let me put it another way. This is discipline within freedom from the bondage of the Law. Now there is no licence to sin here. I know that some of you are saying, 'I'm not very pleased with all this: I don't like the way you are putting it.' I don't care whether you like it or not! This is discipline within freedom, this is the rule, this is the ethic within the theology of grace, and many Christians don't know it. You are living by rules, not by grace. You are not living by the love of Jesus at all. You are constantly sticking up the placard and saying, 'I've done it again.' Of course, you ask His forgiveness, but He says, 'Yes, but you did it because you were looking at the placard; look at Me!'

I want to stress this very much – if you are following me: I'm not sure that you are, all of you. I want to stress this about living a holy, pure life by looking at Christ, not by looking at His Law and the rules. This is discipline within freedom.

I'm going to tell you a story. I don't often see television, or hear it, and no loss, I'm sure, on the whole, but I did hear Tony ... what's his name, Bilbow, isn't it? ... interviewing Danny Kaye, the comedian, in, I think, Late-Night Line-Up. I don't know if Danny Kaye is a Christian but he is a real person, as many of the great comedians are. They can't be real comedians unless they are, that is what makes them funny. They are real, that is where the sense of humour comes in, and some people won't see it, they are so straight-laced and legalistic. Danny hugely embarrassed Tony Bilbow, with his programme gen on his knee, wanting to put Danny into a straight-jacket and go according to the programme as they had planned it. But you can't do that to a chap like Danny.

Danny Kaye was speaking about his life on stage, films, and so on, and the other man said something like this to him: 'You take to yourself a tremendous amount of freedom in your acts; you do it differently each night.' And Danny Kaye said something very interesting in reply. 'Ah, yes,' he said. 'but I exercise that freedom, that "ad libbing" within the strictest theatrical discipline, the most ruthless and rigorous discipline.' And you could see the control amidst the bubbling fun and all that: a master of technique!

Take another illustration. Someone is playing the piano, and he is letting the piano 'have it', and you may think he is just 'bashing away'. Not a bit of it. If you see him coming down with those great crashing Beethoven chords you may not notice that he lifts himself off the seat a fraction of an inch and puts the weight of his whole body (his shoulders and his arms) into that movement. It is not force, it is weight that gives richness, warmth and depth of tone to the volume. That is technique: you see somebody just hitting the piano, as you think, and enjoying himself, and you don't know the technique behind it.

Back to Danny Kaye: it is within the strictest discipline that he exercises the greatest freedom. Now, turn that round for us, for it is not freedom within discipline, as it is for him. For him, or for the pianist, it is learning the technique the hard way. If you are composing music, you must keep to the rules of harmony. If you are writing verse, you must keep to the rules for that. If you are writing prose, you must keep to the rules of grammar, etc. You ought not to be allowed to break out of them and take liberties until you know the rules. You must not break the rules until you know them in practice, and then you will break them intelligently, wisely.

That is not the order for us as Christians; it is not freedom within discipline, it is the opposite order. It is discipline within freedom. It is holiness within grace. It is fulfilling the Law within love, and it is the love that is important, it is the love that enables us to fulfil the Law. We say, 'Lord, I'll do it for You. It hurts me. The old devil is dragging me away to do this horrid thing, but because I love You I can't do it.' Danny Kaye, you see, must attend to his technique because he is a paid comedian. We are not paid comedians, we are children in our Father's house, and we are free. We have the run of the house, but His love is a love – just because of its freedom, just because of its expansiveness – a love that inclines us and constrains us to do the best we can for Him, drawing upon His grace and power.

Now what does this mean for some of you, young people in particular? Are you listening? I hear it said that some young folk around here, from time to time, are too loose in their sexual relationships. I can also believe that, on the other hand, there are some young people so inhibited that they flay themselves alive for the most natural thoughts and physiological passions, and have become so tied up that some of the boys can't look at a girl naturally, or girls at a boy. My problem tonight is that I have these two extreme groups – as well as people in the middle – sitting here before me, and what in the world am I going to say that deals with you all? Would you like to be in my shoes? I'm going to say to you what Paul said to the Galatians, 'For freedom Christ has set us free; stand fast therefore, and do not submit again to a yoke of slavery' (Gal. 5:1). Read also Galatians chapter 5 from verse 13 to verse 25.

Then Galatians 6:1, 2: 'Brethren, if a man is overtaken in any trespass (or fault), you who are spiritual should – throw him out!' Is that what it says? 'You who are spiritual should restore him in a spirit of gentleness. Look to yourself, lest you too be tempted. Bear one another's burdens (that includes our temptations), and so fulfil the law of Christ.'

What am I to say to these two extreme groups? Well, certain things to the one and certain things to the other. First of all, your bodies are Christ's. He has given you your bodies for smiling fellowship with Himself; don't defile them. Other people's bodies are Christ's whether they will or not; don't defile them either. Sex is for marriage. If you want sex, then marry; that is the solution for it (see 1 Cor. 7). If not, not. There are other things to live for, other directions for our powers and passions to take. Ask the married people, they will tell you that.

But there are other questions than this. Someone who is involved very much with young people here and elsewhere, wrote me about some of the problems of young people, and I am going to read now what was written (anonymously, of course).

'I feel that quite a number of young folks have their lines crossed somewhere, and in spite of all the teaching, just don't seem to have the gumption to apply it. You could talk round the why's and wherefore's until you were blue in the face, but I often think that young people today have built up such an image around themselves and the sort of life that is expected, or they think is expected of them, that they are dead scared when someone comes near to unveiling what they really are. Scratch the surface of most of the problems they have and one finds that their basic need is no more and no less than it was a generation ago; only because they have created so many problems in themselves, the digging and scratching are all the harder.'

And in case you think that this is written by a sober-sides, the letter is signed,

'Yours on a soap-box.'

Lines crossed? Does that ring a bell – if I'm not mixing metaphors! I am, but that doesn't matter! No gumption to apply the teaching? I said a moment ago that God's forgiveness is within accepted love. You are first accepted. This is what He says to those who have truly professed their faith: 'You are Mine forever. I will never let you go.' And He has ample forgiveness within that for all our trippings-up and our stumblings and our fallings. And it is within that love of being accepted that you are His and He will never let you go – that He wants you to love Him back, so that you will soon be quite a changed person.

Having said that he offers forgiveness within accepted love, let me say this: He will also offer you thrashings within accepted love; chastenings, discipline within accepted love. Listen to this: 'Have you forgotten,' says the writer to the Hebrews, 'the exhortation which addresses you as sons?' Here you see the Father in heaven putting His hand upon your head and saying, as my dear friend with whom I stayed recently said when he put his hand on the head of his youngster of five years (all dressed up in highland dress because he was going somewhere special that day), 'This is my boy.' It looked so

143

beautiful. 'This is my boy.' It was great!

This is what God is saying through Hebrews: '"My son, do not regard lightly the discipline of the Lord, nor lose courage when you are punished by him. For the Lord disciplines him whom he loves, and chastises every son whom he receives." It is for discipline that you have to endure. God is treating you as sons; for what son is there whom his father does not discipline? If you are left without discipline, in which all have participated, then you are illegitimate children and not sons. Besides this, we have had earthly fathers to discipline us and we respected them. Shall we not much more be subject to the Father of spirits and live? For they disciplined us for a short time at their pleasure (and sometimes with passion), but he disciplines us for our good, that we may share his holiness (which is lovely, and means wholeness, health). For the moment all discipline seems painful rather than pleasant; later it yields the peaceable fruit of righteousness to those who have been trained by it' (Heb. 12:5-11).

Let me say this, very gently. Having made plain to the one side what is required within this love, let us be faithful to it and love Christ so much that we won't grieve Him. But it is the warped, tied-up people with whom I'm more concerned. Let the real love of Christ undo all the bonds, break all the shackles of your tied-up personalities. Relax on Christ, and let your love for Him, responding to His love for you, rise to grown-up love. Let that be the word for both sides, and all those in the middle. Let our love for Him rise to grown-up love, responsible love, and let nothing in the world but love to Jesus try to save us, for it alone will do it, no other. Have we the gumption to apply that? I think that maybe we have.

8

LO, I AM WITH YOU ALWAY, EVEN UNTO THE END OF THE WORLD
Reading: Matthew 28

My text is in the Gospel according to Matthew, chapter 28 and verse 20, the last words in the Gospel: Jesus, the risen Jesus says, 'Lo (look, behold, take note), I am with you always, to the close of the age (or, to the end of the world).' But the first part will do: 'Lo, I am with you.' Not merely, 'You are Mine forever,' that is one thing; but, 'Lo, I am with you alway, even unto the end of the world.'

I particularly want to help some who in the advance of their Christian life come to a stage, sometimes quite soon, sometimes not so soon, when they are gripped with a sense that the Lord has deserted them; and, of course, associated with this (asking the question, 'Why?'), a terrible, paralysing sense of sin. 'It can't be the Lord's fault,' they say, 'it must be my fault.' I want to help such, of whom I'm sure there are many. I want to argue it out with you. Jesus says, 'Lo, I am with you always.' Of course, it has particular reference to going out into the Lord's service, and that is not inapplicable to our situation here, I should think. But first I want to ask, 'Who is it that says this? What right has He to promise it? Is this the Man who said in the Garden,

"Father, if it be possible, let this cup pass from me"? Is this the Man who later on the cross cried out, "My God, My God, why hast Thou forsaken Me?" What right has He to say now, after uttering such wavering words in the two supreme crises of His life, "Lo, I am with you always"?'

Let us be honest. Let us look these three statements in the face. First, we ask in order to understand what right He has to promise this: What was He doing on the cross? Now as we say, and continue to say, Jesus was doing many things in one on the cross. Jesus was taking away our sins. Jesus was bringing to death, to destruction, our sin nature. Jesus was gaining ultimate and everlasting defeat over all the powers of evil. Jesus was providing a potential for us in order that we might enter into many deaths in His death, unto our own resurrections – in this life as well as that which is to come – and unto the resurrections of others who are brought to Christ through our costly and sacrificial service.

But the answer I want to give tonight to the question, 'What was Christ doing on the cross?' is plain and simple, and I want to make it stark. He was suffering the wrath of God for our sins. And it is believed by some that in doing so He was in fact forsaken for a time by His Father. If I may quote from a former minister of mine when I was organist of the Methodist church nearby, the eminent Methodist scholar Vincent Taylor: 'Jesus so closely identified Himself with sinners and experienced the horrors of sin to such a degree that for a time (weigh the words) the closeness of His communion with the Father was broken.'

Notice that Vincent Taylor uses the word 'broken'. I accept the rest of the words. The closeness of the communion with the Father was affected; but he says it was 'broken', so that His face was obscured and He seemed to be (and I'm glad of these words, 'seemed to be') forsaken.

Another scholar, maybe more conservative, says about what happened on the cross when Jesus suffered the wrath of God for our sins: 'Because wrath is no abstract principle, but a personal manifestation, that meant that the unclouded communion with the Father, enjoyed from all eternity, was broken.' A very different man using the same word 'broken'. Then he goes on to say, 'Some commentators have held that He suffered all the pangs of hell in that time, and if hell be at the root an eternity of separation from God, then He assuredly did suffer the pangs of hell in that time.'

Was He forsaken, as He Himself held that He was, quoting the first verse of the Messianic Psalm 22? There are two sides to this. It is impossible that He was objectively separated from His Father. How could He have been actually separated from His Father in doing the very thing that the Father sent Him to do? That would be a queer result of obedience, wouldn't it? After all, Paul tells us, writing to the Corinthians, 'God was in Christ reconciling the world to Himself'; that is, as far as the Father is concerned.

As far as the Spirit is concerned, the writer to the

Hebrews says in chapter 9, verse 14, that it was 'through the eternal Spirit' (notice the word "eternal") that Christ 'offered Himself without spot to God.' The Spirit was in it, and with Him in it.

Are we saying, therefore, that the Father was punishing Christ, venting His wrath upon Christ for our sins on the tree, at the same time as God was in Christ the Son reconciling the world to Himself and while Christ was offering Himself, with the aid of the eternal Spirit, without spot to His God? This would seem to be a flagrant contradiction, a conflict of opposites; yet the only thing we can do is to take the two, however starkly opposite they seem to be, and hold them together, synthesize them, thesis and antithesis, and 'bang' them together and say they are both true, if we are to come to the fulness of the truth and understanding in our heads as well as in our hearts of what Christ was doing, or something of what Christ was doing on the cross.

You logicians must not be afraid of what appear to be contradictions; it is because our minds are too shallow that we cannot see the connection between seeming opposites. If you confine your faith to what you can understand and what you can reason out, you have a poor, poor faith and I wouldn't like to be you in the day of distress and storm. You need to get deeper than that. Let your little rules in the realms of logic and mathematics, etc. apply, but when it comes to this, stretch them to the full: use your reason, think hard in your thinking and reasoning, yes, but own yourself defeated sometimes and say,

'It is beyond me, and beyond my puny little head, or anybody else's puny little head – Einstein, or whoever!' The mighty Apostle, one of the great intellectuals, came to the place where he cried, 'Stop, stop, stop! Don't go any further.' You can't go any further. Admit it, and be conquered by the amazing complexity and paradoxicality of the truth.

Jesus Christ said – not, 'My Father, My father,' but, 'My God, My God, why hast Thou forsaken Me?' Yet He was doing what the Father told Him to do, and the Spirit was with Him helping Him to do it. Surely the sense of separation was a subjective feeling, more intense, of course, than any other human feeling could ever have been, the devil being in it, until for a time He may have seemed to be convinced, if that is possible (this is holy ground and we tread carefully), that His Father was not there. I don't believe that for a moment He thought His Father had changed, any more than He had changed, or had sinned on the cross, else He could never have been raised from the dead; but it seems that He felt Himself to be forsaken.

Was He? Well, God was busy punishing Him, venging His holy wrath upon the sins of men laid on His human body. But objectively, it is impossible that there could have been any real separation. Not only so, but look at the terms of this quote from Psalm 22, 'My God, My God, why hast Thou forsaken Me?' (We will perhaps look at the Psalm later.) He is still addressing the Father as God, My God; don't minimise that.

Then the fact of the 'Why?' He is surprised, in spite of the fact that He knew all he would have to suffer on the tree of punishment, the penalty for men's sins. He is surprised, because there is no ground in Him for all the sins of men that then covered Him, overwhelmed Him, and, as it were, perhaps hid Him from the Father's sight for a time; mountains of human sin upon Him for which He was to be thrashed to death. He knew there was no ground in Him for the Father forsaking Him. He remained the sinless Christ. Although He was 'made to become sin for us' – what words! Oh, Paul, how daring you are – and silly men quibble about it because they are so tiny – how daring you are Paul, to say that Christ was 'made to become sin for us'. But although He was made to become sin for us, yet He remained personally sinless all the way through, else He would not have been raised from the dead.

No man was ever raised from the dead to be immortal. We were speaking this morning about those who had been raised from the dead and died again, like the son of the widow of Nain, and Jairus' daughter, and Lazarus, but no one had ever been raised from the dead as an immortal man, an indestructible human being. He must have been sinless; the resurrection is the proof of it. There is no ground of separation in Him, He was but doing His duty to His Father. Indeed, we know what the Father said about Him; twice He declared from the heavens, 'This is My beloved Son, in whom I am well pleased.' And the Son Himself said, 'I and the

Father are one.' Who could drive a wedge between them? 'Which of you convinceth Me of sin?' He could have had no sense of condemnation when He cried, 'My God, My God, why hast Thou forsaken Me?' He was surprised. Why? Because he had done no wrong to His Father. He was doing His will.

Yes, He was bearing the penalty of men's sins. But Satan was in it. This was a work of Satan. Had not our Lord said earlier in the Garden – and notice these words. There are certain words which for a profound understanding of the Gospel you must integrate into your thinking, certain phrases which you must add to your memory not merely so that you can write them down and quote them, but so that you add to the texture and structure of your thought. Here is one of them, what Jesus said in the Garden, speaking to the devil, or addressing the agents of the devil: 'This is your hour, and the authority of darkness' (Luke 22:53b). I see that even the RSV translates the word 'power'. I wish it would be a bit more accurate, don't you? 'This is your hour, and the authority (not power) of darkness.' As if the Lord said to the devil, 'Go on and do your worst.' In that hour, in the devil's hour, Jesus was led deeper into a subjective sense, a feeling of separation from God His Father, than any other man will ever know.

Now we can see something of our Lord's experience in Psalm 22. Professor R. A. Finlayson has said that you find in the Messianic Psalms the autobiography of Christ, and that is a beautiful statement, which I'm sure is true. Here in Psalm 22 we have a prophetic preview of Christ's anguish on the cross. It begins, as you know: 'My God, my God, why hast thou forsaken me?'

(We must remember, of course, that sometimes it doesn't seem to match up to what we would expect of Christ's autobiography. It was written by the Psalmist, you see, and in a sense is humanly conditioned, yet the truth goes beyond any experience of any mere sinner of men.)

'My God, my God, why hast thou forsaken me? Why art thou so far from helping me, from the words of my groaning? O my God, I cry by day, but thou dost not answer; and by night, but find no rest.

Yet thou art holy, enthroned on the praises of Israel. In thee our fathers trusted; they trusted, and thou didst deliver them. To thee they cried, and were saved; in thee they trusted, and were not disappointed.

But I am a worm, and no man; scorned by men, and despised by the people. All who see me mock at me, they make mouths at me, they wag their heads; "He committed his cause to the LORD; let him deliver him, let him rescue him, for he delights in him!"

Yet thou art he who took me from the womb; thou didst keep me safe upon my mother's breasts. Upon thee was I cast from my birth, and since my mother bore me thou hast been my God. Be not far from me, for trouble is near and there is none to help.

Many bulls encompass me, strong bulls of Bashan surround me; they open wide their mouths at me, like a ravening and roaring lion.

I am poured out like water, and all my bones are out of joint; my heart is like wax, it is melted within my breast; my strength is dried up like a potsherd, and my tongue cleaves to my jaws; thou dost lay me in the dust of death.

Yea, dogs are round about me; a company of evildoers encircle me; they have pierced my hands and feet – I can count all my bones – they stare and gloat over me; they divide my garments among them, and for my raiment they cast lots.

But thou, O LORD, be not far off! O thou my help, hasten to my aid! Deliver my soul from the sword, my life from the power of the dog! Save me from the mouth of the lion, my afflicted soul from the horns of the wild oxen!'

(Psalm 22:1-21)

Then from the twenty-second verse onwards we have the resurrection; the tone is different. Here is Christ among the sons He has gained by His death.

'I will tell of thy name to my brethren; in the midst of the congregation I will praise thee: You who fear the LORD, praise him! all you sons of Jacob, glorify him, and stand in awe of him, all you sons of Israel! For he has not despised or abhorred the affliction of the afflicted; and he has not hid his face from him, but has heard, when he cried to him.

From thee comes my praise in the great congregation; my vows I will pay before those who fear him. The afflicted shall eat and be satisfied; those who seek him shall praise the LORD! May your hearts live for ever!

All the ends of the earth shall remember and turn

to the LORD; and all the families of the nations shall worship before him. For dominion belongs to the LORD, and he rules over the nations.

Yea, to him shall all the proud of the earth bow down; before him shall bow all who go down to the dust, and he who cannot keep himself alive. Posterity shall serve him; men shall tell of the Lord to the coming generation, and proclaim his deliverance to a people yet unborn, that he has wrought it.'

(Psalm 22:22-31)

You see? You have all the agony, you have all the anguish, but you have also the faith, and trust, and looking to the Lord. In fact, you have the positive significance of the 'Why?' It is not right, My God, that Thou shouldest forsake Me, because I put My trust in Thee. Why, then?

We see the same thing – not perfectly, of course – in Job; the darkness of his experience, when God said to the devil one day, 'Look at that fine man of Mine, that righteous man of Mine,' and the devil replied, 'Oh, let me get my hands on him and You will see how fine a man he is, Your righteous Job.' 'All right,' said the LORD, 'within limits I give you permission.' Twice God gave the devil permission, and Job went into a depth of agony beyond speaking. Would you like to read some of Job, so that you may understand how sure we may be that God is with us? Because God is in even the deepest trials.

Here is Job in the midst of an unspeakable trial. You may remember what happened to him. In one day he suffered the loss of all his sons and daughters and all his property. The next day he suffered the most awful sickness, the most loathsome disease imaginable; yet after that it says in Job 2:10, 'In all this Job did not sin with his lips.' In all this Job did not sin with his lips; yet this is what he said in the third chapter, 'Let the day perish wherein I was born, and the night which said, "A man-child is conceived". Let that day be darkness!' (Job 3:3, 4a). 'Why did I not die at birth, come forth from the womb and expire?' (3:11). 'Why is light given to him that is in misery, and life to the bitter in soul, who long for death, but it comes not, and dig for it more than for hid treasures; who rejoice exceedingly, and are glad, when they find the grave? Why is light given to a man whose way is hid, whom God has hedged in?' (3:20-23). 'For the thing that I fear comes upon me, and what I dread befalls me' (3:25). This is psychologically true. 'The thing that I feared comes upon me': that, you see, is inviting Satan. 'I am not at ease, nor am I quiet; I have no rest; but trouble comes' (3:26).

Now read chapters 6 and 7. 'Then Job answered: "O that my vexation were weighed, and all my calamity laid in the balances! For then it would be heavier than the sand of the sea; therefore my words have been rash. For the arrows of the Almighty are in me; my spirit drinks their poison; the terrors of God are arrayed against me"' (6:1-4) ...'Therefore I will not restrain my mouth; I will speak in the anguish of my spirit; I will complain in the bitterness of my soul. Am I the sea, or a sea monster, that thou settest a guard over me? When I say, "My bed will comfort me, my couch will ease my complaint", then thou dost scare me with dreams and terrify me with visions, so that I would choose strangling and death rather than my bones' (7:11-15). Have you ever been in a position when you thought God was dealing with you like that, terrifying you, thrashing you, belabouring you? That is what Job thought, but it wasn't God at all who was doing it, as we read in chapters 1 and 2. It was the devil whom God permitted to test His man Job. 'Then thou dost scare me with dreams and terrify me with visions' (7:14). Job doesn't know; but we know.

Chapter 9: 'Lo, he passes by me, and I see him not; he moves on, but I do not perceive him. Behold, he snatches away; who can hinder him? Who will say to him, "What doest thou?" God will not turn back his anger' (9:11-13a). You see how mistaken he is in his distress. 'How then can I answer him, choosing my words with him? Though I am innocent, I cannot answer him; I must appeal for mercy to my accuser. If I summoned him and he answered me, I would not believe that he was listening to my voice. For he crushes me with a tempest, and multiplies my wounds without cause; he will not let me get my breath, but fills me with bitterness. If it is a contest of strength, behold him! If it is a matter of justice, who can summon him? Though I am innocent, my own mouth would condemn me; though I am blameless, he would prove me perverse' (9:14-20).

Job had a feeling that he wasn't suffering for sin,

and he wasn't. God was testing him. 'Though I am innocent, my own mouth would condemn me; though I am blameless, he would prove me perverse. I am blameless; I regard not myself; I loathe my life. It is all one; therefore I say, he destroys both the blameless and the wicked. When disaster brings sudden death, he mocks at the calamity of the innocent. The earth is given into the hand of the wicked' (9:20-24a). The earth is given into the hand of the wicked. He thinks as we sometimes do about what is happening in the world today. Things are becoming worse; there is so much wickedness abroad. 'He covers the faces of its judges – if it is not he, who then is it?' (9:24b).

Did I not say that it was the devil who was testing him, and he didn't know it? 'If it is not he, who then is it?' Ah, a chink of light. 'If it is not God, who is treating me like this?' Who else could it be? It's the devil; but Job doesn't know it. 'My days are swifter than a runner; they flee away, they see no good. They go by like skiffs of reed, like an eagle swooping on the prey. If I say, "I will forget my complaint, I will put off my sad countenance, and be of good cheer", I become afraid of all my suffering, for I know thou wilt not hold me innocent. I shall be condemned; why then do I labour in vain? If I wash myself with snow, and cleanse my hands with lye, yet thou wilt plunge me into a pit, and my own clothes will abhor me. For he is not a man, as I am, that I might answer him, that we should come to trial together. There is no umpire between us, who might lay his hand upon us both' (9:25-33).

There is no umpire between us – Uh, huh? No daysman? But of course there is. Job didn't know it, but there is Christ. If God is accusing him, then there is an umpire. But it is not God who is accusing him, but the devil.

Chapter 10:1-2, 18-22: 'I loathe my life; I will give free utterance to my complaint; I will speak in the bitterness of my soul. I will say to God, Do not condemn me; let me know why thou dost contend against me.... Why didst thou bring me forth from the womb? Would that I had died before any eye had seen me, and were as though I had not been, carried from the womb to the grave. Are not the days of my life few? Let me alone, that I may find a little comfort before I go whence I shall not return, to the land of gloom and deep darkness, the land of gloom and chaos, where light is as darkness.'

Now over against that, turn to the last chapter of Job, chapter 42. 'After the LORD had spoken these words to Job, the LORD said to Eliphaz the Temanite: "My wrath is kindled against you and against your two friends; for you have not spoken of me what is right, as my servant Job has"' (42:7).

That is what Job thought. That is what God thought. Have you seen a drama on two stages at once, where you have one stage above the other? You see the drama on two levels: so in heaven there is God and Satan, and on earth, Job and his friends. We see both; Job saw the under-stage only.

This is what God says: 'After the LORD had spoken these words to Job, the LORD said to Eliphaz the Temanite: "My wrath is kindled against you and against your two friends; for you have not spoken of me what is right, as my servant Job has. Now therefore ... go to my servant Job ... and my servant Job shall pray for you, for I will accept his prayer not to deal with you according to your folly; for you have not spoken of me what is right, as my servant Job has." So Eliphaz the Temanite and Bildad the Shuhite and Zophar the Naamathite went and did what the LORD had told them; and the LORD accepted Job's prayer. And the LORD restored the fortunes of Job, when he had prayed for his friends; and the LORD gave Job twice as much as he had before' (42:7-10). 'And the LORD blessed the latter days of Job more than his beginning' (42:12). But at the beginning, Job didn't understand what was happening. He thought God was against him, whereas God was only testing him, using the devil.

Now that was what was happening to our Lord – although that was a different, unique category. He *did* know. (You know, don't you, that Christ gained the victory before He died? He exhausted the devil before He died.) Before He died, choosing the moment of His own death, bowing His head, like the King He was, He said these words, 'Father, into Thy hands I commend My Spirit.'

Has He not the right, therefore, to say to you – more right than Job (and he had some right to speak in view of what he had been through) – has this man Jesus not the right to say to you, 'Lo, I am with you always?' And are you not going to take it, and learn with Job and with the Psalmist, patience?

> 'I waited patiently for the LORD; he inclined to me
> and heard my cry. He drew me up from the desolate
> pit, out of the miry bog, and set my feet upon a rock,
> making my steps secure. He put a new song in my
> mouth, a song of praise to our God. Many will see
> and fear, and put their trust in the LORD. Blessed is
> the man who makes the LORD his trust, who does not
> turn to the proud, to those who go astray after false
> gods!' (Psalm 40:1-4).

This is the word concerning those to whom in
the fulness of time, when they have gone on a little
way in the Christian life, the Lord says, 'Ah, he is
getting on. He is making some progress. I must test
him.' And He withdraws the felt sense – are you
heeding my words? – He withdraws the felt sense
of His presence, and says to Satan, 'Careful now;
have a go, but within these limits!' And as soon as it
happens, we say, 'Oh, what have I done to deserve
this? I have sinned, but I don't know my sin. I know
that I am a sinner all the time, but I haven't sinned
specifically. I haven't committed any of the heinous,
flagrant sins. Why has this happened to me? God
has gone. All the nice feelings I had when I was first
converted have gone. O God, it doesn't work. I've
been deceived; it has been a dream. It has been a
mere emotional experience.' Not a bit of it!

May I tell you something? I find Isaiah 26 very
precious, because, as many people here know, in
past days, before I came to this church, I had a lot

of nervous, psychological, even mental trouble, and I did wonder sometimes if it would not be better to end it all; but I knew I couldn't, because God had been real to me, and I knew He had a purpose for my life. We used to sing a choir piece of some of these words in Isaiah 26, and the words are amongst the most precious in the whole Bible to me. I have lain tossing a whole night, with never a wink of sleep – sometimes for weeks – clenching my hands and looking at the dark, then at the twinkling lights of Aberdeen, and back to bed again, writhing and clenching, thinking, Oh, God, how long can this go on? And underneath I heard the choir which I used to conduct, singing, 'Thou wilt keep him in perfect peace, whose mind is stayed on Thee; because he trusteth in Thee'.

However deep the distress, and however dark the dungeon, if we know we are His, we know it must end, just as if we heard the footsteps of someone coming along the corridor of the prison to open the door and set us free to step out into the light. We hold on to that. But the difficulty is, it is not only the anguish of feeling that God has deserted us and left us to our foe, but the conviction of sin which comes with it. 'I have sinned. He is grieved with me. He has departed from me.' You may have sinned, but listen – be very careful! – it doesn't matter even if you have; because if you have sinned, there is a remedy. Confess your sin. 'If we walk in the light, as he is in the light, the blood of Jesus Christ keeps cleansing us from all sin'; so that, as Paul tells the Romans (8:1), 'There is now no condemnation.' My brothers and sisters, I want to say something daring here. Even when sin is involved (and when Satan comes, there is bound to be some sin), you are still not to be condemned. Run to God the Father and confess. Rather, run to the Son, the Advocate.

1 John 1:5-10: 'This is the message we have heard from him and proclaim to you, that God is light and in him is no darkness at all. If we say we have fellowship with him while we walk in darkness, we lie and do not live according to the truth; but if we walk in the light, as he is in the light, we have fellowship with one another, and the blood of Jesus his Son cleanses us from all sin. If we say we have no sin, we deceive ourselves, and the truth is not in us. If we confess our sins, he is faithful and just, and will forgive our sins and cleanse us from all unrighteousness. If we say we have not sinned, we make him a liar, and his word is not in us.'

Run to the Advocate. Say, 'Lord Jesus Christ, what did You do for me?' Tell Him that He spilt His blood for you. Tell him quickly. You mustn't lose the sense of His presence; because there is no condemnation. Even when you have been tripped up by the devil, when you have been tripped up by someone else, or even by yourself, there is no condemnation. That doesn't mean we have licence to sin, you know that perfectly well.

I don't know if I would say this absolutely, but in the context of what I have been saying, I think we might take it nearly absolutely: God is nearest when we don't feel Him; that is, of course, in our time of need. And faith, realising this, maintains trust, and even may in a very objective sort of way enjoy communion in the darkest, most unfeeling hour. The one you have to be most careful of is the accuser of the brethren – the devil! (Rev. 12:10)

When you come to Jesus Christ, and your sins are pardoned and God says, 'There is now no condemnation to those who are in Christ Jesus', then you are to believe that, and you are never, never to believe that God has deserted you simply because you have been tripped up. Never, *never!*

If for a time you don't feel His presence and your heart does not condemn you and there is nothing to confess – if there is, of course, get busy and attend to it – but if there is nothing to confess, say, 'God has a purpose in this. He has put out a few lights for a purpose. I will wait patiently in my dungeon; they will come on again. He is coming; He is coming; He will come. He promised, "Lo, I am with you always." He is coming. He will put them on again. I will not doubt. I will not doubt. I will not doubt, but *Trust!*'

9

FATHER FIGURES
Reading: Hebrews 12

Father figures: Hebrews 12:9, 10. Let us take in the
sense of these two verses, and note that I am dealing
not with the whole argument of the passage say from
5 or 6 to 11 which is the question of discipline –
chastisement if you like – but I am dealing simply
with what we find in verses 9 and 10, a comparison
of earthly fathers, however good or not so good,
with our heavenly Father who is here singularly (for
this is not found anywhere else in the Scriptures)
called the Father of spirits.

'We have had earthly fathers to discipline us and
we respected them. Shall we not much more be
subject to the Father of spirits and live?' (v.9). The
words I pick out are 'much more', 'Shall we not
much more be subject to the Father of spirits and
live?' Our subjection to Him is unto life, for – notice
the connection – they (our earthly fathers) disciplined
us for a short time (in childhood and youth) at their
pleasure, according to their whim, or according to
their lights, if you like; but He disciplines us for our
good, unerringly, and never makes a mistake as the
best earthly father can do. You see the comparison?
'For they disciplined us for a short time at their
pleasure, but he disciplines us for our good, that we
may share his holiness' (v.10).

Now as I say, I want to restrict our consideration to these two verses and a comparison of the discipline of earthly fathers (standing over to protect, or dominate, or both) with our heavenly Father and his liberating Fatherhood.

As to our earthly fathers or father figures, it need only be stated to be apparent, that to speak to some folk of God as our heavenly Father, is repulsive to them; it is really anathema, because, as they have grown up, they have learned to hate their fathers; and if God is a Father, then they don't want Him. They have had enough of fathers. That is not true of everyone, but it is true of some. I want to show the harm that is done in respect of this; and I must do it delicately, and pray God to give me wise and balanced words, certainly helpful words. Many need this word, and I hope I can give it truly and helpfully. I want to show the harm that is done both by over-dominant and over-protective parents in comparison with what I have called the liberating Fatherhood of God.

There is a true earthly fatherhood which is to be honoured. We have that, of course, in the fifth commandment. 'Honour thy father (notice the word "honour") and thy mother: that thy days (note what it says; "that thy days") may be long upon the land which the LORD thy God giveth thee' (Exod. 20:12, AV). Many a man and woman have had their lives cut short because they have failed to honour and care for their parents. 'That is the first commandment with a promise,' says Paul. He writes of it in his letter to the Ephesians, and he uses a sterner word than the word 'honour' which the commandment uses, 'Children, *obey* your parents in the Lord, for this is right' (6:1). Then he quotes from the fifth commandment, 'Honour your father and mother ... that it may be well with you and that you may live long on the earth' (6:2, 3). Then he says (and we will come to it), 'Fathers, do not provoke your children to anger, but bring them up in the discipline and instruction of the Lord' (6:4). There is also a parallel passage in Paul's letter to the Colossians (3:21), where he says simply, 'Fathers, do not provoke your children, lest they become discouraged.'

This indicates that there is a true earthly fatherhood to be honoured. Of course the best earthly fathers, natural and spiritual (some of us are fathers who have no natural children, and that is one of the highest privileges in the world), seek to relate and attach their children properly, firmly, wisely to their heavenly Father.

You find that even in the Old Testament. Listen to David. When David's time to die drew near, he charged Solomon his son, saying, 'I am about to go the way of all the earth. Be strong, and show yourself a man, (this to Solomon!) and keep the charge of the LORD your God, walking in his ways and keeping his statutes, his commandments, his ordinances, and his testimonies, as it is written in the law of Moses, that you may prosper in all that you do and wherever you turn; that the LORD may establish his word which he spoke concerning me, saying, "If your sons take heed to their way, to walk before me in faithfulness with all their heart and with all their soul, there shall not fail you a man on the throne of Israel'" (1 Kings 2:1-4).

Solomon himself, having been so wisely taught by his father, seeks to teach his sons also; and one of the first things he teaches in the book of Proverbs is, 'The fear of the Lord is the beginning of knowledge; fools despise wisdom and instruction' (Prov. 1:7). Then he says (Prov. 2:1-8), 'My son, if you receive my words and treasure up my commandments with you, making your ear attentive to wisdom and inclining your heart to understanding; yes, if you cry out for insight and raise your voice for understanding, if you seek it like silver and search for it as for hidden treasures; then you will understand the fear of the Lord and find the knowledge of God. For the Lord gives wisdom; from his mouth come knowledge and understanding; he stores up sound wisdom for the upright; he is a shield to those who walk in integrity, guarding the paths of justice and preserving the way of his saints.'

Again Solomon says (Prov. 3:1-4), 'My son, do not forget my teaching, but let your heart keep my commandments; for length of days and years of life and abundant welfare will they give you. Let not loyalty and faithfulness forsake you; bind them about your neck, write them on the tablet of your heart. So you will find favour and good repute in the sight of God and man.'

'Trust in the LORD with all your heart, and do not rely on your own insight.' Did you hear that? 'In all your ways acknowledge him, and he will make straight your paths. Be not wise in your own eyes; fear the LORD, and turn away from evil. It will be healing to your flesh and refreshment to your bones' (3:5-8).

'Honour the LORD with your substance (what you make and what you produce) and with the first fruits of all you produce; then your barns will be filled with plenty, and your vats will be bursting with wine' (3:9, 10).

'My son, do not despise the LORD's discipline or be weary of his reproof, for the LORD reproves him whom he loves, as a father the son in whom he delights' (3:11, 12).

You see, the Old Testament too has an idea of the Fatherhood of God; it is not very pronounced, but it is there, although it is in our Lord Himself that the Fatherhood of God is so supremely and perfectly revealed.

Listen to what the Psalmist (David again) says of the Fatherhood of God in relation to the possible neglect or failure of earthly parents: 'When my father and my mother forsake me, then the LORD will take me up' (Psalm 27:10, AV). And listen to a passage from Isaiah 42, which, although it doesn't speak of God as Father – it really speaks of God as Messiah, Christ – yet the whole passage is suffused with the grace of Fatherhood, the gentle, loving care of the true Father in heaven: 'Behold my servant, whom I uphold, my chosen, in whom my soul delights; I have put my Spirit upon him, he will bring forth justice to the nations (and he will do it gently). He will not cry or lift up his voice, or make it heard in the street; a bruised reed he will not break, and a dimly burning wick he will not quench.' He will support the weak: He will not trample on them. 'He will faithfully bring forth justice. He will not fail or be discouraged till he has established justice in the earth; and the coastlands wait for his law' (Isa. 42:1-4).

Lastly, we have the same spirit in Jeremiah. '"At that time, says the LORD, I will be the God of all the families of Israel, and they shall be my people." Thus says the LORD: "The people who survived the sword (that is, in Jerusalem, in the destruction of Jerusalem, presumably) found grace in the wilderness."' Babylon! God came to them in Babylon, and blessed them in the wilderness! Then He says this, 'When Israel sought for rest, the LORD appeared to him from afar.' And this is what He said, 'I have loved you with an everlasting love; therefore I have continued my faithfulness to you' (Jer. 31:1-3).

Israel herself at certain times recognises the good Fatherhood of God, and recognises her need of such a Father in times of stress. Israel is crying out through the prophet Isaiah, 'Look down from heaven and see, from thy holy and glorious habitation. Where are thy zeal and thy might? The yearning of thy heart and thy compassion are withheld from me' (Isa. 63:15). Then the prophet says, 'For thou art our Father, though Abraham does not know us and Israel does not acknowledge us; thou, O LORD, art our Father, our Redeemer from of old is thy name' (Isa. 63:16). Again, 'Yet, O LORD, thou art our Father; we are the clay, and thou art our potter; we are all the work of thy hand. Be not exceedingly angry, O LORD, and remember not iniquity for ever. Behold, consider, we are all thy people' (Isa. 64:8, 9).

Lastly, under this head, what the New Testament says about the Fatherhood of God. Our Lord shows to perfection the grace, love, tenderness and liberating power of the Father. Read John's Gospel. Read the passages where Jesus speaks so wonderfully about His Father. Read especially chapters 14 to 17.

Then hear what the apostle Paul says in 2 Corinthians 6: 'As God said, "I will live in them and move among them, and I will be their God, and they shall be my people. Therefore (because He has given them this vast promise, that He will live among them and move among them and that they shall be his people) come out from them (the heathen), and be separate from them, says the Lord, and touch nothing unclean; then I will welcome you" – and notice this – "and I will be a father to you, and you shall be my sons and daughters, says the Almighty"' (2 Cor. 6:16b-18). Notice these words, weigh them: 'And I will be a father to you.' He is our heavenly Father.

Jesus Himself in the Lord's Prayer taught us to say this: 'Our Father, who art in heaven.' But God has a chance of being a Father only to those who let

Him be a Father to them, and this is His appeal. In a sense, this is the Gospel appeal: through His Son Jesus Christ, He is holding out His hands to you and me, saying, 'Will you let me be your Father?' And He has given us the right to reply, 'No,' if we want to. Wonderful, and terrible!

So much for our heavenly Father. What about earthly fathers? They, says the writer to the Hebrews, discipline us according to what seems good to them, according to their whim and passion and temper: He for our profit. Is that a hard thing to say about fathers? Let us take this broadly and in balance: we are a fallen race, fathers and children alike, and the evil bias we inherited from our first parents through the Fall and through the devil, affects everything and everybody. It is in this sense that the ancient scholars and godly men spoke about our total depravity, meaning that depravity, rebellion, perversity, the perversity of the human will, which enters into every department of our life. As it affects the natural world, much more it affects creatures with minds and wills, especially man, the crown of creation.

That applies to our fathers, the best of them, and because of that Job tells us that, 'Man is born to trouble, as the sparks fly upwards' (Job 5:7). Man is 'born in sin'. Again the Psalmist tells us, 'Behold, I was shapen in iniquity; and in sin did my mother conceive me' (Psalm 51:5). Even Eve's deliverance from her share of guilt from the Fall, her deliverance through child bearing, is qualified. 'For Adam was formed first, then Eve; and Adam was not deceived, but the woman was deceived and became a transgressor. Yet woman will be saved through bearing children, if' – the 'if' is all important for my point here – 'if she continues in faith and love and holiness, with modesty' (1 Tim. 2:13-15).

Because of the Fall, the dice is loaded absolutely against us. We are born in sin and shapen in iniquity and there are far more chances, the grace of God apart, that things will go wrong with us than that they will go right; in fact, they are bound to go wrong, because they are all wrong from the beginning. It is due to what we call the common grace of God that we do not descend into a complete sink of iniquity, into a demonic hell. Man is kept because of God's purpose of gathering His Church and building His kingdom. Man is preserved from the worst effects of his disobedience.

I want you to think about this. As a child is the product of its heredity and environment, these affect it before it is born. They affect pregnancy, and the growth in the womb. They particularly affect birth, the circumstances, and the unconscious experience of the unsuspecting infant in birth. That is why (and I speak very solemnly and with chastity), that is why there is tremendous need for parents to cover the whole circumstances and activity of producing children with prayer.

Think what we have read about Mary in the Magnificat, when the angel had pronounced that she was to be the mother of our Lord. She said, 'How can this be?' And the angel answered, 'I will tell you

173

how it will be, and how He will be such a marvellous child.' (This is what we are to pray for in the conception and birth of our children.) 'The Holy Spirit will come upon you.' – It touches my heart to say it. – 'The Holy Spirit will come upon you, and the power of the Most High will overshadow you; therefore the child to be born will be called holy, the Son of God' (Luke 1:34, 35).

A friend of mine, seeking to understand himself – it is a whole-time occupation seeking to understand ourselves; how much harder for other people to understand us, don't you think? – a friend, seeking to understand himself, the quirks and all that, was directed to read a little from Dr. Frank Lake, the psychiatrist, and he learned that it is very possible that the warps and twists which develop in our lives may have something to do with a bad birth, or having been deprived of the protection and care of a nursing mother in the first months of life. The dear chap inclined to pooh-pooh the whole thing as ridiculous, in spite of the fact that he had problems. Then he discovered that he had had a very bad birth and that the first few months of his life were spent in hospital. I don't know that that proves anything, but it certainly suggests a good deal. But you see the importance of these things. The only way to be safe in marriage and in child bearing is to live as close to God as Mary was living to God, so that He keeps everything as right as possible, and keeps the enemy, and all evil and sin, as far away as possible.

I recall as a young man being intrigued in my

folly and, I suppose, frivolity, when told by an older man that the conception of his children was covered with prayer. But was that wrong, when you think of the conception, for good or evil, of an infant? You can certainly see the vital importance of all these things, especially the early months and years of our lives, and what it may cost a human personality ultimately to have been deprived of protection, nursing and care in infancy and in childhood. That is why there are so many today (because of the sin in the world and in the nation) who are mis-made; that is why hospitals for people with mental and psychological diseases are crammed full. It is sin that is mis-making so many and, due to no fault of theirs in the first instance, they live with an evil inheritance the whole of their lives.

It is a plain fact that an infant needs, not only wants but needs, to cling to his mother's breast. Before that lovely couple, who came to us the other weekend from the American Air Force, and who had been converted in Germany through an American Padre – a friend of ours, since returned to the United States – before they left for Weisbaden, the wife said, 'I'm longing to get back. You see, I express my love to my children.' (They have five; two boys and triplets, two girls and a little boy, and naturally they are very proud of their family.) 'I give my children a lot of loving. I sometimes give them other things, too, but I give them a lot of loving.' I thought, 'What a wise parent! No stint in her loving, no inhibition about expressing it.' We dour Scots are so slow, aren't we? Granite! God help us. I admire that about her, and it taught me a lot.

Now children are usually older than one can, wisely, do that to. Perhaps there are different ways of doing that to older children, but, my, if I were a natural parent, I think I see what would be needed. Very likely there are some of you here tonight, warped because you were not protected as much as you ought to have been when you were very young; and it may be that you have grown up with what the psychiatrists would call feelings of rejection, which have persisted perhaps from infancy or childhood. Responsibility for that may not lie with your parents, because of their circumstances; but it could. What a responsibility; it makes one almost afraid to be a parent, natural or spiritual.

Then what follows for so many unhappy children, not wanted enough in infancy and in childhood, not cared for enough? Mothers not seeing motherhood as a single vocation, but something by the way as the mere fruit of indulgence, legitimate though it be; failing to regard motherhood as a vocation right through, at least, to beyond adolescence. Then when the children grow into their teens, the neglect, the lack of love and care, security and protection, often run to a kind of parental domination, a desire to over-organise the children, to tyrannise them, to knock them into their particular shape, as if they were making pieces of furniture. They even use them for their prestige: 'What my boy can do,' and, 'What my girl can do': even use them as a vicarious fulfilment for all their unfulfilled parental ambitions. 'I never got to University, but my son will get to University whether he is fit for it or not.' Madness, madness! Too many at University, aren't there? Some should be plumbers, joiners – and lots of other things of more use than some of the things stuffed into ordinary heads today.

Not wanted in childhood, but then when they grow up they are to be perfect little paragons, perfect little machines, objects of admiration; as if we can make them that by not wanting them, and then wanting to dominate them. One main reason why many young folk are so maladjusted, is that children become wrongly related to their parents, and whether it is their parents' conscious fault or not, the fact remains.

You have, on the one hand, children who grow up to be far too dependent, tied to their mother's apron strings, clinging to their mother's breast when they are far beyond that age; never maturing, incapable of independent choice and mature, manly life in the world. And on the other hand, children who become over-dominated, dragooned personalities that have been ironed out. You know, this sometimes applies to mothers more than fathers; dominating madams, amazons of the home, who absolutely iron out their sons and make them either feeble little yes-men ('Yes, Mummy!'); or, if they are too strong-willed to suffer that, make them rebellious; like those youngsters who caused so much trouble in the London School of Economics. My, how they needed a thrashing! Wasn't there a man in that college to give these two little brats a good thrashing? It isn't done, of course, we don't thrash, but we need to sometimes, when it comes to that. Then when people come to their senses, as I think many today will need to come to their senses, we can then show them the love they need. But they need to be restrained.

Well, I have shown you the two extremes, the two products of childhood and youth, in which children are wrongly related to their parents: on the one hand, overprotected, too dependent, and on the other, over-dominated. The Word of God has something to say to each of those.

To the first, those who can't grow up and won't grow up, and cling to their parents in wrong ways, ways that hinder their growth and development into manliness and womanliness and independence – true independence – Jesus says, 'If any one comes to me and does not hate his own father and mother and wife and children and brothers and sisters, yes, and even his own life, he cannot be my disciple. Whoever does not bear his own cross and come after me, cannot be my disciple' (Luke 14:26). You don't like the word 'hate'? Jesus uses the word deliberately to shock, and maybe you need to be shocked, if you are in a condition of sickly dependence on your parents. He says, 'If any one comes to me and does not hate his own father and mother and wife and children and brothers and sisters, yes, and even his own life, he cannot be my disciple.'

Then in the Gospel according to Matthew: 'He who loves father or mother more than me is not worthy of me' (Matt. 10:37a). I believe there are some young people who, perhaps, partly dislike the idea, for they know that they almost worship their parents. It won't do, and the Lord gives us a very stringent word about it.

Take the other side, and it is with this that I am more concerned. Take those who have been – and I find that they are very much in the majority – over-dominated by their parents. Paul has a word for it and I read it a moment ago. It is to the parents, of course, first of all. 'Fathers, do not provoke your children, lest they be discouraged.'

This is also expressed very fully in the New Testament, not in terms of fatherhood, although it applies thus, but in terms of a legalism that the New Testament, and our Lord and the Apostles renounce. So we are back again to an old haunt. In this context perhaps too, you would like to follow me as I read Romans 7. Read this in relation to over-dominant parents, from whom we are not able to break free. 'Do you not know, brethren – for I am speaking to those who know the law – that the law is binding on a person only during his life? Thus a married woman is bound by law to her husband as long as he lives; but if her husband dies she is discharged from the law concerning the husband. Accordingly, she will be called an adulteress if she lives with another man while her husband is alive. But if her husband dies she is free from that law, and if she marries another man she is not an adulteress' (Rom. 7:1-3).

'Oh,' you say, 'but that doesn't apply.' Oh, but we will make it apply! For purposes of Christian growth and development, it is necessary to set aside the injurious, or baneful influence of an earthly father or mother, and find another Father who will understand better and who will liberate our personalities, even our Father who is in heaven. You can call the first father, the Law, and the second Father, grace, and that is the same thing.

Paul says in Romans 7:5, 'While we were living in the flesh, our sinful passions, aroused by the law, were at work in our members to bear fruit for death.' Don't you see that one of the most injurious things is, that when we are over-dominated, when we are bossed too much by someone and not allowed the full, free, legitimate expression of our lives, it makes us mad. Many a son or daughter has gone astray because he or she has rebelled against too strict an upbringing; and that is exactly what the Apostle says here, that when the law is imposed, it puts the very devil into us. Sin and the devil see to that.

Romans 7:6: 'But now we are discharged from the law.' That is to say, 'Now we have a better Father, One who will neither be over-indulgent, nor over-strict.' 'We are discharged from the law, dead to that which held us captive, so that we serve not under the old written code but in the new life of the Spirit.'

I believe with all my heart that it has been necessary, it has been in the will and plan of God for some of you to get away from home, much as your parents may be anxious about you and how you live and what you do, so that you may get a chance to fulfil yourselves.

Let me go on from the second half of Romans 7:7: 'If it had not been for the law, I should not have known sin.' (This is what the law does, this is what strictness does.) 'I should not have known what it is to covet if the law had not said, "You shall not covet." But sin, finding opportunity in the commandment, wrought in me all kinds of covetousness. Apart from the law sin lies dead. I was once alive apart from the law, but when the commandment came, sin revived and I died; the very commandment which promised life proved to be death to me. For sin, finding opportunity in the commandment (these are the important words), deceived me and by it killed me. So the law is holy ...' (Rom. 7:7b-12a). Let me be careful here. Our fathers laid down the law for our good, there is no doubt about that; but laying down the law is not the way to bring up a boy or a girl. Yes, there must be some laying down of the law, but within the context of grace; and it is the grace that tells, not the law. The law has to be hidden in the grace.

Let us go back: the beginning of the Bible is not law, although the Old Testament is full of law: the beginning of the Bible, the first eleven chapters of Genesis, indeed the whole of it, is grace, grace, grace; the grace of God's promises to Abraham – no conditions. God just says, 'I'm going to do this good thing to you, and I'm going to do that; and give you this, and that!' That is grace, without conditions. There are conditions later on, of course (the circumcision for Abraham, and so on), but they are of less importance; they are not unimportant, but they are given in the context of free, sovereign grace. 'Here you are,' says God (this is what loving parents ought to do more often), 'Here you are, I give you all the grace and all the love unconditionally.'

There are rules, but the trouble with so many is that the rules are sometimes more important than the children. God sometimes lets His children go astray. It might be better sometimes to let our children go astray a little if they will, rather than hold them in and make them worse. I know that is dangerous doctrine. I know that all I am saying is dangerous, but I don't deny it on that account. The law is holy and the commandment is just and good. Did that which is good then bring death to me? No! Don't blame the law; by no means. It is sin to blame. It is not that our parents, laying down the law, are wrong, but we are such sinners that the law puts the devil into us, and it is not the best way to make us work. The way to make us work is to use grace, with law in that context; there has to be law, but it is certainly not the whole and certainly not the dominant thing.

Now a little bit of Galatians to the same effect – a marvellous passage, 4:21-31, which tells the same story under other figures. 'Tell me,' says Paul, 'you who desire to be under law, do you not hear the law? For it is written that Abraham had two sons, one by a slave and one by a free woman. But the son of the slave was born according to the flesh, the son of the free woman through promise.' (He was a miracle son, born in their old age.) 'Now this is an allegory: these women are two covenants. One is from Mount Sinai, bearing children for slavery; she is Hagar. Now Hagar is Mount Sinai in Arabia; she corresponds to the present Jerusalem (legal Jerusalem, Pharisaical Jerusalem), for she is in slavery with her children (the Pharisees). But the Jerusalem above is free, and she is our mother (our father, too!). For it is written, "Rejoice, O barren one that dost not bear; break forth and shout, thou who art not in travail; for the desolate hath more children than she who hath a husband."

'Now we, brethren, like Isaac, are children of promise (grace). But as at that time he who was born according to the flesh persecuted him who was born according to the Spirit, so it is now. But what does the scripture say? "Cast out the slave and her son; for the son of the slave shall not inherit with the son of the free woman." So brethren, we are not children of the slave but of the free woman.' God is our Father and His Fatherhood is a liberating Fatherhood.

'For freedom Christ has set us free; stand fast therefore, and do not submit again to a yoke of slavery. Now I, Paul, say to you that if you receive circumcision, Christ will be of no advantage to you (that is, as a law). I testify again to every man who receives circumcision that he is bound to keep the whole law. You are severed from Christ, you who would be justified by the law; you have fallen away from grace (to fall into legalism).' To fall into legalism is to fall away from grace. Will we ever get that into our heads? I doubt it; but it is true. 'For through the Spirit, by faith, we wait for the hope of righteousness. For in Christ Jesus neither circumcision nor uncircumcision is of any avail, but faith working through love. You were running well; who hindered you from obeying the truth? This persuasion is not from him who called you. A little leaven leavens the whole lump. I have confidence in the Lord that you will take no other view than mine; and he who is troubling you will bear his judgment, whoever he is' (Gal. 5:1-10).

God's love is shown to us in this, that He says, 'I have only one requirement of you. *Love Me back.*' That is why the little girl threw away her doll. She ran to Mummy, and Mummy said, 'Why have you thrown away your pretty dolly?' 'Oh Mummy, she won't love me back!'

Love Him back – and our neighbour as ourselves. This is what James calls 'the royal law, according to the scriptures'. They say that Martin Luther thought the epistle of James was a bit legalistic. Had he missed 1:25 and 2:10 when he said that? Perhaps, just for a moment. Dear old Martin Luther!

Listen to what the epistle of James says about this law of love: It is 'the royal law, according to the scripture' (Jas. 2:8). And he also calls it – this is choice, delicious – he calls it, 'the perfect law of liberty'. There is a paradox, if you like. 'He who looks into the perfect law, the law of liberty ... shall be blessed' (Jas. 1:25).

Now I want you very definitely to begin to work this out in your lives. I want you to think it over, to think it out in a right way that doesn't violate the Christian commandment to honour our parents. That must not be broken. Think it out in a right way, a way that God will give us grace to follow; for we must learn so to attach ourselves to our heavenly Father that we are liberated both from overprotection and from over-domination. If we let that seep into our inner beings and let the blessed Gospel of the Fatherly love of God take hold of us, some of us will be much more liberated personalities. It will cost. It may cost a great deal in various ways. It always costs a great deal to put things right, but the worth of it will be untold.

Here is the Gospel then, to every one. Break out from your prisons, dear folk – every prison – into the liberating Fatherhood of God; for that alone will save us in an evil generation. God help us!

10

THE FATHERHOOD OF GOD;
A FATHER OF THE FATHERLESS
Reading: Psalm 68, particularly verses 5 and 6

Now, to the theme of the ministry recently. I am astonished at how often there is more than a connection between what we are finding in the morning in our readings in Colossians and what the Lord gives to me to say in the evening. Over many years now the Lord has led us through various schemes of teaching and there have been times when for months the theme has been pretty nearly the same, and we have been thoroughly indoctrinated by the Spirit and by the Word upon it.

It is a burden on my heart at this time that we should know, understand and profit from the doctrines of God's grace; grace as the essence of the Gospel, unmerited love. It is a weak way to speak of it really, because the grace of God is so overwhelming that it takes the whole of God's holy Word and all the power of the Holy Spirit to bring it home to our cold, dark, unresponsive hearts. I am so very, very sure that a great many of the problems we try to deal with in other ways, on other levels, by resolutions of one kind or another, setting the strictures of God's Word before us, are wrong, in that we haven't really begun to learn that that is not the way to grow in grace, character and maturity. I will never tire of saying this – using the words 'saved' and 'salvation' in their progressive sense, largely – it is only love that saves.

We know that love can be grim, and we have shown from the Word of God through the years a very great deal of that, far too much for some people; but it is, nevertheless, true that the heart of the matter is in God's sovereign, regal grace. So I want to speak this evening for a little about the Fatherhood of God, and I want to be as practical and helpful as I can; and, of course, I want to bring it out from the Scriptures. I want to show you from the Scriptures, from beginning to end, that this is a Book of the grace of God, and of the offer and promise of God's fatherly grace to those who respond to the Gospel message and avail themselves of the salvation that is in Jesus Christ.

I don't want to go back this evening to any comparison between our heavenly Father and earthly fathers and mothers; that caused some a little pain last Sunday, which, I suppose, was natural. I don't think we were unfaithful, or unfair, but I don't want to go back over that; simply to say that whatever sort of father and mother we have (and the word 'father' can cover all sorts of guardians, can't it?), there is only one Father who can really save us.

You know what I mean by save. I don't mean necessarily that one goes to a meeting or a Gospel mission and makes some kind of assent to the Gospel; signs a card, or goes out to the front or undertakes some outward action, and is then saved. I have no doubt that many are saved that way, but that is only the beginning of the salvation that goes on and on and on, and is completed when we receive our resurrection bodies. We won't be fully saved until then, but we have to learn an awful lot about the grace of God in these mortal, aching bodies we were speaking of in prayer a moment ago.

I want to take the word here in Psalm 68, and the fifth and sixth verses: 'Father of the fatherless and protector of widows is God in his holy habitation. God gives the desolate a home to dwell in; he leads out the prisoners to prosperity; but the rebellious dwell in a parched land.' But I don't want to take the text only, but the most of the psalm, because I am concerned with the Fatherhood of God for His people, Israel, which is a type of His Fatherhood for us who believe in His name and receive His Son. I want to take it in the whole sweep of God's leading His people out of Egypt, although that is scarcely mentioned in the psalm, out into the wilderness to Sinai, where He gave them the Law and said it was unto life, if they could keep it perfectly. Then through the wilderness, and their tortuous windings until all the disobedient and rebellious generation of adults died out; and in thirty-nine years all the children entered into Canaan by the side entrance round the Dead Sea.

What we are concerned with this evening is God our heavenly Father leading His people from Sinai to Zion, from the Law to grace in Jesus Christ. There is a great deal in the psalms about this. If you care to turn to Psalms 120 to 134, you find that they are called in the Revised Standard Version (which I am using), Songs of Ascent. They are all Songs of Ascent, and they are all songs that Israel sang going up in procession to Jerusalem to worship.

Take Psalm 121, 'I will lift up my eyes to the hills.' What are the hills? The hills of Zion. From whence does my help come? My help comes from the Lord, who is coming to hover over Zion and over the Ark and the Tabernacle. We know Psalm 121 very well.

Look at the marvellous Psalm 122: you may remember Parry's version of it, which has been sung now at a few coronations, that marvellous, marvellous anthem: 'I was glad when they said to me, "Let us go to the house of the Lord!" Our feet have been standing within your gates, O Jerusalem!' (vv. 1, 2). 'Pray for the peace of Jerusalem! "May they prosper who love you! Peace be within your walls, and security within your towers!"' (vv. 6, 7).

And in Psalm 124, when they reach the place of safety, the fortress of Zion, they say, 'If it had not been the LORD who was on our side, let Israel now say – if it had not been the LORD who was on our side, when men rose up against us, then they would have swallowed us up alive' (vv. 1-3a). Read them through some time, all those psalms (120 to 134) describing Israel on her way to Zion, where God had made His home, where He sought to make His home amongst His people.

Now let us think for a moment about the contrast

between Sinai and Zion, the Law (the Ten Commandments) and the Gospel of the grace of God in Jesus Christ. Turn again to a very interesting portion of Scripture which we read last Sunday, Galatians 4:21-31: 'For it is written that Abraham had two sons, one by a slave and one by a free woman ... But what does the scripture say? "Cast out the slave and her son; for the son of the slave shall not inherit with the son of the free woman." So, brethren, we are not children of the slave (children of the Law; we are not under the Law but under grace) but of the free woman.'

And the conclusion of the matter: 'For freedom Christ has set us free; stand fast therefore, and do not submit again to a yoke of slavery' (Gal. 5:1).

You see, it is up from Sinai with the Law, which is unto life, if you can keep it perfectly, but if you can't keep it perfectly, it is unto death and condemnation. It is up from there to Jerusalem, which comes down from above and doesn't demand holiness and righteousness of us, although it wants us to have it. It gives it. If God requires you to be holy (and He does), He doesn't say, 'Be holy in your own strength. Go on. Be holy!' We cannot. We have broken the Law. We can't do any more. He gives us holiness; and holiness is Jesus Christ.

We can look at it another way. Here is a fascinating hymn by John Keble, which we often sing. It describes the contrast (and you find it in the epistle to the Hebrews also), between Sinai and the thunderings and lightnings there, and Jerusalem and Pentecost.

When God of old came down from heaven,
  In power and wrath He came;
Before His feet the clouds were riven,
  Half darkness and half flame.

But, when he came the second time,
  He came in power and love;
Softer than gale at morning prime
  Hovered His holy Dove.

The fires that rushed on Sinai down
  In sudden torrents dread,
Now gently light, a glorious crown,
  On every sainted head.

And, as on Israel's awe-struck ear
  The voice exceeding loud,
The trump that angels quake to hear,
  Thrilled from the deep, dark cloud.

So, when the Spirit of our God
  Came down His flock to find,
A voice from heaven was heard abroad,
  A rushing mighty wind.

It fills the Church of God; it fills
  The sinful world around;
Only in stubborn hearts and wills
  No place for it is found.

Come, Lord; come, Wisdom, Love, and Power;
  Open our ears to hear;
Let us not miss the accepted hour;
  Save – (His saving power, you see, not ours)
  Save, Lord, by love or fear.

Do you see what God is seeking in all this? In taking Israel from Egypt into the wilderness to Sinai and giving them the Law and the Tabernacle and all that, then taking them through the wilderness by a tortuous route to Zion, He is taking them home. He is taking them to His home, and until they are there, He cannot be at home. He protects them with the pillar of fire by night and the pillar of cloud by day in the wilderness, but He is impatient to get home. No father worth his salt would be glad to get home if his bairns weren't with him. So He waits until He can take them home. He is seeking a dwelling place for Himself and them.

I am going to give six texts (three of them in Revelation). We start with Exodus 25:8. Listen to what God says so early in the Old Testament: 'And let them make me a sanctuary, that I may dwell in their midst.' Exodus 29:45, 46: 'And I will dwell among the people of Israel, and will be their God. And they shall know that I am the LORD their God, who brought them forth out of the land of Egypt that I might dwell among them; I am the LORD their God.' Notice, 'I will dwell among the people of Israel and will be their God.'

Now when Solomon completed the building of his temple (2 Chron. 7), the priests prepared to go in and worship God according to the Levitical rituals and the sacrifices – but what did they find? 'When Solomon had ended his prayer (a long prayer in the sixth chapter of 2 Chronicles), fire came down from heaven and consumed the burnt offering and the sacrifices, and the glory of the LORD filled the temple. And the priests could not enter the house of the LORD because the glory of the LORD filled the LORD's house. When all the children of Israel saw the fire come down and the glory of the LORD upon the temple, they bowed down with their faces to the earth on the pavement, and worshipped and gave thanks to the LORD, saying, "For he is good, for his steadfast love endures forever." Then the king and all the people offered sacrifice before the LORD' (2 Chron. 7:1-4).

The next text is in the New Testament, in John 14:23 and it is wonderful. Jesus said to His disciples, 'If a man loves me, he will keep my word, and my Father will love him ...' I love this, I think this is choice – 'and we will come to him and make our home with him.' Now that is God's desire expressed in a word; that is what he wants to do, to make His home amongst His people, His church, to be happy there and for them to be happy there.

2 Corinthians 6:16b-18, quoting from the Old Testament: 'As God said, "I will live in them and move among them, and I will be their God, and they shall be my people. Therefore come out from them (the heathen), and be separate from them, says the Lord, and touch nothing unclean; then I will welcome you, and I will be a father to you, and you shall be my sons and daughters, says the Lord Almighty."'

But the best is to come. Revelation 3:20: 'Behold,' says Jesus by the Spirit, 'I stand at the door (of your heart) and knock (Christ knocking at the door of the

Church's heart): if any one hears my voice and opens the door, I will come in to him and eat with him, and he with me.' I will stay, I will 'bide' with him.

Revelation 7:15-17: 'Therefore are they before the throne of God, and serve him day and night within his temple (the redeemed ones, that is); and he who sits upon the throne will shelter them with his presence. They shall hunger no more, neither thirst any more; the sun shall not strike them, nor any scorching heat. For the Lamb in the midst of the throne will be their shepherd, and he will guide them to springs of living water; and God will wipe away every tear from their eyes.' Can you think of anything more comforting than that?

Revelation 21:3, 4: 'And I heard a great voice from the throne saying, "Behold, the dwelling of God is with men. He will dwell with them, and they shall be His people, and God Himself will be with them." He says it again: "He will wipe away every tear from their eyes, and death shall be no more, neither shall there be mourning nor crying nor pain any more, for the former things have passed away." '

That is what God made the worlds for, that He might have a nice home for Himself with His bairns. That is it; the sum of it. It is His pleasure to be with His people whom He has redeemed in Jesus Christ. In fact, the Psalmist in Psalm 132 cries out in the midst of the psalm, 'Arise, O LORD, enter into thy rest' (v.8). 'You are tired, LORD. You have come from Egypt. You have come from Sinai. Come. LORD, find rest in Your own home in Zion.' We cannot really rest until we are at peace, and that is where He wants to rest, and resting there, hovering over His people, watching over them, as He is watching over us tonight. He is hovering for our protection.

Would you like to look at the 91st Psalm? It is great. 'He who dwells in the shelter of the Most High ...' It is almost like the figure of a hen spreading her wings to protect her chicks from enemies. Jesus Himself uses that figure later on. And in many places in the psalms, the Psalmist speaks of God spreading out His wings to protect His people. 'He who dwells in the shelter of the Most High, who abides in the shadow of the Almighty, will say to the LORD, "My refuge and my fortress; my God, in whom I trust." For he will deliver you from the snare of the fowler ... When he calls to me, I will answer him; I will be with him in trouble, I will rescue and honour him. With long life I will satisfy him, and show him my salvation' (Psa. 91:1-16).

One other passage, the prophecy of Hosea; we are coming to something different here. We have not only the assurance that God will remain with His people, that it is His pleasure to abide with His people, but the assurance that He will never let them go; they are his forever. ('I have loved you with an everlasting love; therefore I have continued my faithfulness to you,' see Jer. 31:3.) Israel of old was very faithless to God, and in Hosea chapter 11 the Lord puts into the heart and mind of Hosea (who himself was a very tender, gentle, patient, loving man, much more than Amos), something of the feelings and mind of the Almighty for His children when they stray from Him, because He wants to protect them and bless them. It begins like this:

'When Israel was a child, I loved him, and out of Egypt I called my son.' (That was the beginning of the nation.) 'The more I called them, the more they went from me; they kept sacrificing to the Baals (the false gods), and burning incense to idols. Yet it was I who taught Ephraim to walk, I took them up in my arms; but they did not know that I healed them. I led them with cords of compassion,' (Isn't that an interesting phrase?) '... I led them ... with the bands of love, and I became to them as one who eases the yoke on their jaws (their horses, or donkeys, or cattle), and I bent down to them and fed them' (Hos. 11:1-4).

But He is grieved with them almost to anger. 'They shall return to the land of Egypt, and Assyria shall be their king, because they have refused to return to me. The sword shall rage against their cities, consume the bars of their gates, and devour them in their fortresses. My people are bent on turning away from me; so they are appointed to the yoke (foreign yoke as captives), and none shall remove it' (Hos. 11:5-7).

So God sends them away into captivity. But He can't put up with it. He puts them out of His house, and like the father of the prodigal son, He can't get a minute's peace. He can't sleep, He can't eat, He can't do anything! And in one of the most moving passages in the whole of the Old Testament, He cries out – here is our heavenly Father broken-hearted because His people won't shelter under His love – 'How can I give you up, O Ephraim! How can I hand you over (to your enemies), O Israel! How can I make you like Admah! (one of the cities which went down with Sodom and Gomorrah). How can I treat you like Zeboiim! My heart recoils within me (against doing that).' (God says, 'There is a great revulsion in My heart against putting you out and keeping you out. I can't stand it.') 'My compassion grows warm and tender. I will not execute my fierce anger. I will not again destroy Ephraim; for I am God and not man, the Holy One in your midst, and I will not come to destroy' (Hos. 11:8, 9).

His forgiveness of His children whom He has loved with an everlasting love, is perpetual. Seventy times seven? Seven million times seven! He goes on forever forgiving His children, however wayward they are. Oh, He thrashes them sometimes, puts them out, as we see, but never lets them go; and He forgives them and forgives them, and forgives them. And His forgiveness, His constant forgiveness, is a sign to us of the unending and undeviating love of God. Why, He even says through the apostle Paul, 'While we were yet sinners Christ died for us' (Rom. 5:8).

And so he stands on the watchtower, the Father of the prodigal son, and peers out into the distance; and the legalistic, self-righteous, pharisaic, elder brother is no comfort to Him, for all his outward righteousness. He wants that boy! He is His boy, and He won't let him go, and He will stand there until He sees him in the distance.

Now, my friends, this is the salvation of God. This is the power of grace that is given to us to make us Christ-like, and happy, and useful, and glorious to God. And I want to spend the little time that is left to me to find how we can realise this in our lives. How we can derive the benefit of this love that goes on loving, and will go on loving and loving, right to the very end!

Well, it is spiritual. Spiritual things are spiritually discerned. You won't find it merely in the thinking of your reason. Nothing wrong with that, but you won't find it there. You won't find it in the movings of your emotions, your sentimental, or your sad, or your elated, or your excited emotions; you won't find it there.

Do you remember that after the resurrection, when Mary Magdalene realised it was Christ and not the gardener who was standing before her in the Garden, she cast herself at His feet and would have clutched Him? But He said to her, 'Touch me not.' Now, that may mean several things, and perhaps it means them all, but it means this: 'Mary Magdalene, and James and Peter and John, and all the rest of you, for the next forty days I'm going to appear before you suddenly through closed doors, and up in Galilee at the Resurrection Picnic, and on the road to Emmaus; and I'm going to stay with you for a little time, and then disappear as suddenly as I appeared; and you are not to touch Me (apart from Thomas feeling My bones to see that I am not a ghost.) You are not to touch Me, and you are not to have Me very long at any one time during these forty days, because I, the real, risen Christ, am only flitting into your presence and out again, to teach you to trust Me spiritually, and not to depend on these poor fleshly eyes of yours, but upon the eyes of your heart, the eyes of faith that God gives to His own children. For, "Lo, I am with you, always!"'

I think, you know, that many of us are greatly put off our spiritual stride because we always want nice feelings. We equate nice, warm, happy, comfortable feelings with the presence of God, and when we don't feel nice, we think He has gone. Sometimes He is nearer when we don't feel nice, and sometimes He wants us not to feel nice. Is that perverse and cruel? Not a bit of it. He wants to train us to trust in His constant presence.

This is spiritual, and we have got to let the spiritual truth of all these blessed words I have given soak into our minds. We have got to meditate upon them as the Lord said to Joshua, and as the Psalmist speaks of in the long psalm (Psa. 119). 'Oh, how I love thy law! It is my meditation all the day.... How sweet are thy words to my taste.'

The Word of God, written down upon the page, black upon white, has to become experience in our human flesh; not in a fleshly sense, but in a spiritual sense, for we are spiritual beings. The truth that I have read so much of this evening, has to become faith to believe that it is true, whatever we feel. It is as we believe that it is true, that the power of the Spirit through the Word seeps and soaks into our minds, and saturates our beings. Have I not seen generations of young believers grow up in Jesus Christ because they have done this? I have the evidence in hundreds of people who have been soaked in the truth, who have really believed that God loves them, and have known that that is the most important thing they can know.

Let us take the word Paul writes in First Thessalonians. Writing to those whom he loves very much, he says, 'May the God of peace himself sanctify you wholly' (1 Thess. 5:23a). What he means there is something like this: 'May the God who is peace, and who gives peace, deep deep peace which affords stability of character, which nothing else in the world can produce, and a sense of grace, a sense of well-being because God is good and He is over all and is guiding us and leading us out; may the God of peace Himself come down by His Spirit and drench us and almost drown us in His grace, and sanctify us, and set us apart for God's pleasure, wholly, utterly.'

Then Paul goes on to say in the next breath, 'And may your spirit and soul and body be kept sound and blameless at the coming of our Lord Jesus Christ' (1 Thess. 5:23b). Let me take that a moment, 'May your spirit and soul and body ...' I have read various scholarly articles in which the scholars have discussed whether man's nature is bi-partite or tri-partite, whether he is soul and body, or spirit and soul and body. Of course, he has a spirit. I believe that man is bi-partite, is body and soul, or soul and body; but if you use the word 'spirit' we know perfectly well what that speaks about; that speaks about the spiritual part of man. We sometimes call it the soul, but when the apostle Paul here uses the three, he is, I think, drawing from the first and the third to find that area of our bi-partite body and soul, body and spirit if you like, which forms the emotional part of us, the sensitive part of us, the part of the senses. So the Apostle says, 'May your spirit and soul and body be kept sound and blameless at the coming of our Lord Jesus Christ.' That is to say: May you be saturated in the spirit of God's grace, in the wonderful truths of His loving Fatherhood, this Fatherhood of love that will never let us go and keeps forgiving and forgiving us.

One other word, and it is a great word. The first two verses of Romans 12, where the Apostle says, 'I appeal to you therefore, brethren, by the mercies of God, to present your bodies as a living sacrifice, holy and acceptable to God.' Present your bodies to God – the whole of your life to God as a living sacrifice. What does that mean? Living for Him, not living for yourself, because to live for Him means to live to be the very best you can be, and enjoy it. You gain your life by losing it. Jesus says, 'present' – 'hand over'. The word is sometimes said to mean a conquered soldier or soldiers surrendering arms. That is it.

'I appeal to you therefore, brothers, by the

mercies of God, to present your bodies as a living sacrifice, holy (that is, set apart for God) and pleasing to God, which is your spiritual (or logical, or reasonable) worship.' Then he says this, 'Do not be conformed to this world.' You are a spiritual being. If you have received the Spirit of Jesus Christ, you belong to another world and you can live rightly as a Christian in this world only when you are drawing upon the resources of God's grace from the other world, when you are allowing the overshadowing glory, love and grace of God to envelop you, protect you, bless you and use you. '... but be transformed by the renewal of your mind, that you may prove what is the will of God' – for you; which is good, pleasing to him, and perfect in its accomplishments.

There is nothing in which we are so sorely needing renewal of our minds as in the fact of the grace of God. His loving care. We must have another think about that. The trouble is, we won't let Him love us as He wants. And if we let Him love us a little, we say, 'That was nice, Lord. How much do I pay?' That is right! That is the kind of creatures we are – commercial! We live in that world. 'What does it cost?' we say, reaching for our pocket book. And when our Father in heaven says, 'There is nothing to pay,' we are insulted. We don't like to be patronised. That is our pride, that is our fallen-ness.

Will you get rid of your rotten pride, and let God love you? *Really* love you, forgive you, over and over again, until it saturates you so much that all the warpedness, all the twisting, all the 'snorrels', all the tangles will become unravelled? Then more and more you will become sweet, patient, cheerful, easy-to-live-with souls, because you are not nursing, as secret, something that is trying desperately to be something it can't be. You are not running away into a corner, saying, 'I'll please God my own way!' – It is like running into a dungeon or cave and putting on our flash lamp, when the sun is blazing outside. Aren't we silly? Aren't we? Bovine, indeed! O God, help us to let You really love us.

And of course, it is only when we begin to let God really love us, that we begin to love people. You cannot begin to love people until you know how you have been loved. If you have no experience of being loved, you are not able to love anybody else; you don't know how to do it. You can make the outward motions, but what is the good of that? You have got to let Him really love you, favour you, indulge you with His grace. Rest in it, bask in it, a thousand times a day.

Now do take it in. This is one of the most practical things I could say to you. You must learn to live in this realm, and as you do, you will truly be transformed, and people will see it, and they will want it too – some of them, at least. May God grant it.

Books by William Still
available from Christian Focus

Dying to Live
ISBN 0 906 731 97 6   B format 192 pp

In his own words, William Still describes his
upbringing in Aberdeen, his ill health as a young
person, and his call to the ministry. Then he highlights
aspects of church life to which he has given
prominence – including expository preaching, music
in worship, and children in the church. Written when
he was eighty years old and still preaching in his
own congregation, this book is an insight into the
worldwide influence of his ministry.

Towards Spiritual Maturity
ISBN 185792 0155   B format 64pp

In this book William Still considers the path to
Spiritual Maturity, a path that involves living in the
shadow of the cross. 'This is a book to be read and
re-read, to be applied constantly and shared with
others. It will serve as a key to open the treasure
store of good things' (Sinclair Ferguson).

MENTOR TITLES

Creation and Change by Douglas Kelly (large format, 272 pages)
A scholarly defence of the literal seven-day account of the creation of all things as detailed in Genesis 1. The author is Professor of Systematic Theology in Reformed Theological Seminary in Charlotte, North Carolina, USA.

The Healing Promise by Richard Mayhue (large format, 288 pages)
A clear biblical examination of the claims of Health and Wealth preachers. The author is Dean of The Master's Seminary, Los Angeles, California.

Puritan Profiles by William Barker (hardback, 320 pages)
The author is Professor of Church History at Westminster Theological Seminary, Philadelphia, USA. In this book he gives biographical profiles of 54 leading Puritans, most of whom were involved in the framing of the Westminster Confession of Faith.

Creeds, Councils and Christ by Gerald Bray (large format, 224 pages)
The author, who teaches at Samford University, Birmingham, Alabama, explains the historical circumstances and doctrinal differences that caused the early church to frame its creeds. He argues that a proper appreciation of the creeds will help the confused church of today.

MENTOR COMMENTARIES

1 and 2 Chronicles by Richard Pratt (hardback, 520 pages)
The author is professor of Old Testament at Reformed Theological Seminary, Orlando, USA. In this commentary he gives attention to the structure of Chronicles as well as the Chronicler's reasons for his different emphases from that of 1 and 2 Kings.

Psalms by Alan Harman (hardback, 420 pages)
The author, now retired from his position as a professor of Old Testament, lives in Australia. His commentary includes a comprehensive introduction to the psalms as well as a commentary on each psalm.

Amos by Gray Smith (hardback, 320 pages)
Gary Smith, a professor of Old Testament in Bethel Seminary, Minneapolis, USA, exegetes the text of Amos by considering issues of textual criticism, structure, historical and literary background, and the theological significance of the book.

Focus on the Bible Commentaries

Genesis – John Currid
Exodus – John L. Mackay*
Deuteronomy – Alan Harman*
Judges and Ruth – Stephen Dray
1 and 2 Samuel – D. Ralph Davis*
1 and 2 Kings – Robert Fyall*
Proverbs – Eric Lane (1999)
Daniel – Robert Fyall
Hosea – Michael Eaton
Amos – O Palmer Robertson*
Jonah-Zephaniah – John L. Mackay
Haggai-Malachi – John L. Mackay
Matthew – Charles Price
Mark – Geoffrey Grogan
John – Steve Motyer (1999)*
Romans – R. C. Sproul
2 Corinthians – Geoffrey Grogan
Galatians – Joseph Pipa*
Ephesians – R. C. Sproul
Philippians – Hywel Jones
1 and 2 Thessalonians – Richard Mayhue (1999)
The Pastoral Epistles – Douglas Milne
Hebrews – Walter Riggans
James – Derek Prime
1 Peter – Derek Cleave (1999)
2 Peter – Paul Gardner (1998)
Jude – Paul Gardner

Journey Through the Old Testament – Bill Cotton
How To Interpret the Bible – Richard Mayhue

Books in bold are currently available.
Those marked with an * are currently being written.